How to Write a Police Report

HOW TO WRITE A POLICE REPORT

S. Dennis Miller

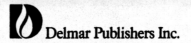 Delmar Publishers Inc.

Notice to the Reader

Publisher does not warrant or guarantee any of the products described herein or perform any independent analysis in connection with any of the product information contained herein. Publisher does not assume, and expressly disclaims, any obligation to obtain and include information other than that provided to it by the manufacturer.

The reader is expressly warned to consider and adopt all safety precautions that might be indicated by the activities described herein and to avoid all potential hazards. By following the instructions contained herein, the reader willingly assumes all risks in connection with such instructions.

The publisher makes no representations or warranties of any kind, including but not limited to, the warranties of fitness for particular purpose or merchantability, nor are any such representations implied with respect to the material set forth herein, and the publisher takes no responsibility with respect to such material. The publisher shall not be liable for any special, consequential, or exemplary damages resulting, in whole or in part, from the readers' use of, or reliance upon, this material.

Cover design by Berg Design

Delmar Staff
Senior Administrative Editor: Vernon Anthony
Project Editor: Carol Micheli
Production Coordinator: Barbara A. Bullock
Art Supervisor: Judi Orozco
Design Coordinator: Karen Kemp

For information, address Delmar Publishers Inc.
3 Columbia Circle, Box 15-015
Albany, New York 12212

Printed in the United States of America
published simultaneously in Canada
by Nelson Canada,
a division of The Thomson Corporation

2 3 4 5 6 7 8 9 10 XXX 99 98

Library of Congress Cataloging-in-Publication Data

Miller, S. Dennis.
    How to write a police report / S. Dennis Miller.
        p.   cm.
    Includes index.
    ISBN 0-8273-4728-6
    1. Police reports.   I. Title.
HV7936.R53M55 1993   92-36440
808'.066363—dc20   CIP

TABLE OF CONTENTS

ILLUSTRATIONS

PREFACE

▼

Since 1970 I have read thousands of police reports as a deputy district attorney. It was apparent to me early in my career — as I am sure it is apparent to any prosecutor — that narrative police reports are a critical part of the evaluation of criminal cases, of the decision of what charge to bring, and of the trial of a criminal case. I have prosecuted almost every type of crime, have questioned every type of witness, and have won my share of cases. I also have been battered and beaten by astute defense attorneys who, like good counterpunchers, have taken advantage of every opening.

The police officer's narrative report has been one of the most common sources of such openings for a defense attorney. My experience with police reports has shown me that when an officer's narrative reports are well written, the officer's court appearances are fewer, cross-examination is less vigorous, and the defense attorney concedes more facts. Well-written police reports also tend to result in more appropriate convictions and sentences.

The question, then, is What makes a well-written narrative police report?

This text describes a specialized format for writing all types of narrative reports. City police, deputy sheriffs, and state troopers in Oregon have successfully used this format for a number of years for original crime reports as well as for follow-up reports. The format has been used with different types of investigative activities, e.g., crime scene processing, interviews with suspects and witnesses, undercover operations, and the execution of search warrants. This format has also been used with different types of crimes: from crimes against persons to property crimes, from drug and vice crimes to crimes against the government.

There have been many books and manuals written on the subject of writing police reports. Most of them deal with simplifying the language used by police officers in their reports, and with explaining how to write clearly. Unfortunately they also urge officers to focus on collecting and reporting the facts, i.e., *who, where, what, why, when, how,* etc.

The premise of this text is that narrative police reports should be witness oriented rather than fact oriented. Facts are of little importance unless they can be presented in court. During the investigation, police officers collect facts by talking to people who have firsthand information. Officers also notice facts firsthand, thereby becoming witnesses themselves. Clearly, witnesses are indispensable to the fact-collecting process during the investigation. Facts cannot be collected without witnesses, and facts must not be reported without linking them to witnesses.

This text describes a method for writing the narrative section of any type of police report in a way that meets the needs of those in the criminal justice system who rely on that report. In particular it meets the needs of the prosecutor in evaluating criminal cases, in bringing the correct charges, and in obtaining the correct resolution to the case.

I believe that an officer who uses this method for writing narrative reports will satisfy all departmental needs as well as the needs of supervisors, other officers, support personnel, and others in and outside of the criminal justice system. This method also may prevent defense attorneys from misusing the police report as a means of attacking the state's case instead of as the source of accurate information it was intended to be. It is my hope that the suggestions contained in the following pages will be adopted by police officers. Implementing these suggestions will make it easier for officers to write reports, for other people to read and understand those reports, and for prosecutors to convict those who commit crimes.

Narrative police reports, like any other tool of a police officer, are most effective when used exactly and exclusively for the job for which they were designed. The purpose of the narrative police report is to communicate the results of every investigation in a manner that satisfies the needs of those who work in the criminal justice system. The power of a well-written narrative police report is as awesome as any weapon in its impact on those who commit criminal acts.

S. Dennis Miller
Chief Deputy District Attorney
Clackamas County, Oregon

ACKNOWLEDGMENTS

▼

I am in debt to the countless municipal police officers, deputy sheriffs, and state troopers who have used this method over the years to write their reports and who have discussed with me various problems of report writing. I am also grateful to the hundreds of criminal justice students and police officers to whom I have taught the report writing method described in this text. By their comments and criticisms and by their questions these officers and students have slowly shaped and honed the method that now appears in this text.

I also want to thank my fellow prosecutors. Their comments and frustrations about police reports in cases they were handling gave me valuable insights into narrative police reports.

Not to be ignored are those defense attorneys who taught me about weaknesses in narrative police reports by their relentless probing for soft spots in the cases I tried against their clients.

Without the contributions of these professionals this text could never have been written.

A special thank you is owed to J. Dyanne McDuna, a remarkable and talented friend who spent countless hours editing and proofreading the many stages of this text. Her dedication, humor, helpful criticism, and patience were the catalysts for this text.

I wish to recognize some very helpful people who were kind enough to read this text's manuscript. Their constructive criticisms were very much appreciated. They are Clackamas County District Attorney James W. O'Leary, Deputy District Attorney Terry Gustafson, West Linn Police Chief Terry Hart, Alan Kreutzer, and Terrie Walker. I wish to thank Thomas Kusturin, an investigator for the Clackamas County District Attorney's Office, for his ideas and suggestions that led to the chapter on note taking. I also thank Clackamas County Deputy Sheriff Bob Davis for his advice, support, and interest.

Several others must be recognized for their support and encouragement over the years that this text was being developed. They are Durwood Thomas, an instructor in Criminal Justice at Portland Community College, Captain Lee Erickson of the Oregon State Police, and Detective Jon Alford of the Clackamas County Sheriff's Office.

I also wish to acknowledge and thank the following reviewers for their helpful comments and suggestions.

To each these people, a heartfelt thank you!

REVIEWERS

Elmer Criswell, Jr.
Harrisburg Area Community College
Harrisburg, Pennsylvania

Robert J. Dompka, Ph.D.
Montgomery College — Rockville Campus
Rockville, Maryland

Frank L. Fischer
Kankakee Community College
Kankakee, Illinois

Michael Grimes
Southeast Florida Institute of Criminal Justice
Miami, Florida

Thomas Lenahan
Herkimer County Community College
Herkimer, New York

Philip A. Ludos
Washtenaw Community College
Ann Arbor, Michigan

Verne H. McClure
Auburn University at Montgomery
Montgomery, Alabama

Norman J. Raasch
Lakeland Community College
Mentor, Ohio

Stephen Vizvary
Broome Community College
Binghamton, New York

Terry Walker
Trinidad Jr. College
Trinidad, Colorado

David Whelan
Western Connecticut State University
Danbury, Connecticut

James E. Zink
Fulton Montgomery Community College
Johnston, New York

CHAPTER ONE

▼

The Importance of Police Reports

1.1 WHO READS THEM

People who work in the criminal justice system read police reports as part of their job. They are involved in the system from arrest through the correctional process. They read police reports to get information that helps them make decisions in their jobs.

Other officers read reports to guide their own investigative activities, e.g., interviewing, evidence gathering, making arrests, etc. Police supervisors review reports to determine case assignments and to evaluate the investigating officer's ability, knowledge, and performance. Officers from other police agencies may read reports related to cases in their own jurisdiction, e.g., car theft rings, serial murders, multiple burglaries or rapes, etc.

Records clerks read reports for indexing, filing, and extracting statistical data. Many police departments also employ personnel who analyze police reports for repetitive patterns in criminal activity so that road patrol schedules can be changed, surveillance activities begun, or suspects identified.

Prosecutors read reports to assess the strengths and weaknesses of the case and to decide what charges to file. Prosecutors also prepare for trial by reviewing the police reports to decide which witnesses are needed to prove the case, what questions to ask, and which physical exhibits to use. They use these reports to determine which defenses to anticipate and thus plan case strategy. Once criminal charges are filed, defense attorneys read the police reports to decide whether to plea bargain a case, argue for a lighter sentence, file a motion to suppress evidence, or go to trial. In preparing for trial, defense attorneys review police reports to plan trial tactics, cross-examination of witnesses, and arguments for the judge and jury.

Judges read police reports to decide legal questions regarding such issues as probable cause for searches and the admissibility of evidence. At the time of sentencing, police reports may be submitted to the judge to help determine what the appropriate sentence or conditions of probation should be.

Corrections officials use police reports to determine appropriate conditions of parole or probation as well as to recommend the level of incarceration and supervision.

Others whose skills or expertise are used in the criminal justice system also read police reports to make recommendations or give advice. Such people include mental health professionals, accident reconstruction specialists, and forensic pathologists. Others with special skills, like drug and alcohol abuse counselors, may also rely on police reports to make decisions about the appropriate level of treatment.

People who work outside of the criminal justice system read police reports. Insurance agents may read police reports to decide questions of liability and damages. Many administrative agencies have staff who read police reports to determine whether to recommend denial of licenses or whether certain regulations have been violated.

All people who read police reports have one thing in common; each expects to take some action or make a decision based on the word picture created by the police report. It is common for that action or decision to have severe economic or punitive consequences for individuals and for society and its institutions.

Of all those who read police reports, probably the most critical readers are prosecutors. Their decisions are bound by precise and stringent constitutional and statutory laws, and often have serious and far-reaching consequences for people and for society. The police report is the critical link between the police function and the prosecution function. For the criminal justice system to work effectively and efficiently, that link must remain strong.

CITY OF TUALATIN
Police Department
INCIDENT REPORT

1 CASE NUMBER	2 CONNECT CASE NO		ACCOMPANYING REPORTS: CUSTODY / EVIDENCE / CONTINUATION / ACCIDENT	PAGE ___ OF ___
3 OFFENSE			4 DAY OF WEEK OCCURRED: 11 SUN / 13 TUE / 15 THUR / 17 SAT / 12 MON / 14 WED / 16 FRI / 18 UNK	
5 LOCATION OF OCCURRENCE		6 DATE/TIME REPORTED	7 DATE/TIME OCCURRED	

PERSONS   V VICTIM   W WITNESS   C COMPL   R OWNER   K DECEASED   I RUNAWAY   B PARENT   ADD'L PERSONS Y N

8 CODE	9 NAME LAST FIRST MIDDLE	10 SEX	11 RACE	12 DOB
13 HOME ADDRESS			14 HOME PHONE	
15 BUSINESS/SCHOOL ADDRESS		16 WORK HOURS	17 BUSINESS PHONE	
18 CODE	19 NAME LAST FIRST MIDDLE	20 SEX	21 RACE	22 DOB
23 HOME ADDRESS			24 HOME PHONE	
25 BUSINESS/SCHOOL ADDRESS		26 WORK HOURS	27 BUSINESS PHONE	
28 CODE	29 NAME LAST FIRST MIDDLE	30 SEX	31 RACE	32 DOB
33 HOME ADDRESS			34 HOME PHONE	
35 BUSINESS/SCHOOL ADDRESS		36 WORK HOURS	37 BUSINESS PHONE	

VEHICLE   1 - ARRESTEE S   2 SUSPECTS   3 - DAMAGED   4 EVIDENCE   6 SAFEKEEPING   8 RECOVERED   9 - STOLEN   0 - OTHER

38 CODE	39 YEAR	40 MAKE	41 MODEL	42 STYLE	43 COLOR(S)	44 VIN	45 VALUE
46 LICENSE	47 LIC STATE	48 LIC YEAR	49 LIC TYPE	50 AUTH USE Y N	51 DEL PAY Y N	52 KEYS IN Y N	53 DRIVEABLE Y N	54 BODY DAMAGE Y N

55 TOWED BY/TO		56 REASON	57 AUTHORIZED BY

58 PRIV REQ / DEPT REQ	59 HOLD Y N	60 REASON	61 INVENTORIED BY	62 UNIT/PERSON NOTIFIED

CRIME ANALYSIS

TYPE OF STRUCTURE   [ ] N/A

63 Non Residental
- 1 Convenance
- 2 Tavern/Bar
- 3 Restaurant
- 4 Fast Food
- 5 Drug/Medical
- 6 Gas Station
- 7 Retail Store
- 8 School
- 9 Financial Inst
- 10 Vehicle
- 11 Public Building
- 12 Warehouse
- 13 Industrial
- 14 Office
- 15 Construction
- 16 Other

64 Target(s)
- 1 Cash Reg/Drawer
- 2 Owner-Employee
- 3 Safe-Box
- 4 Vending Machine
- 5 Display Items
- 6 Storage Area
- 7 Customer
- 8 Other

65 Residental
- 1 Sgl Family Dwelling
- 2 Apt
- 3 Condo
- 4 Duplex
- 5 Hotel/Motel
- 6 Other

66 Target(s)
- 1 Basement
- 2 Bedroom
- 3 Den/Family Rm
- 4 Garage/Carport
- 5 Living Room
- 6 Storage Area
- 7 Kitchen
- 8 Person
- 9 Other

67 METHOD OF ENTRY
- 1 Attempt Only
- 2 No Force
- 3 Key/Slip
- 4 Body Force
- 5 Saw/Drill/Burn
- 6 Hid in Bldg
- 7 Channel Lock
- 8 Pipe Wrench
- 9 Tire Iron
- 10 Brick/Rock
- 11 Unkn Pry Bar
- 12 Bolt Cutters/Pliers
- 13 Punch
- 14 Window Smash
- 15 Tape/Wire
- 16 Screwdriver
- 17 Lock Box
- 18 Unlocked
- 19 Other

68 POINT OF ENTRY   [ ] N/A
- 1 Unknown
- 2 Front
- 3 Rear
- 4 Side
- 5 Grl Level
- 6 Up Level
- 7 Door
- 8 Window
- 9 Sliding Glass
- 10 Duct Vent
- 11 Adj Bldg
- 12 Roof/Skylight
- 13 Wall
- 14 Garage
- 15 Basement
- 16 Trunk/Hood
- 17 Other
- 18 Ext

69 SUSPECT ACTIONS
- 1 Occupied building
- 2 Unoccupied building
- 3 Indication of mult suspects
- 4 Vandalized
- 5 Ransacked
- 6 Neat
- 7 Smoked on premises
- 8 Ate/drank on premises
- 9 Used matches for light
- 10 Alarm disabled/bypassed
- 11 Disabled phone
- 12 Shut off power
- 13 Prepares exit(s)
- 14 Vehicle needed to remove property
- 15 Used lookout driver
- 16 Knew location of hidden property
- 17 Selective in property
- 18 Took victim s vehicle
- 19 Used victim s tools
- 20 Stashed property
- 21 Suspect armed
- 22 Fired weapon
- 23 Demanded money
- 24 Used demand note
- 25 Placed property in sack/pocket
- 26 Struck victim
- 27 Inflicted injury
- 28 Made threats
- 29 Threatened retaliation
- 30 Bound/gagged victim
- 31 Blindfolded victim
- 32 Ripped/cut clothing
- 33 Forced victim to move
- 34 Required victim to act
- 35 Molested victim
- 36 Used victim s name
- 37 Impersonated other
- 38 Hideout technique
- 39 Unusual odor(s)
- 40 Masturbated
- 41 Disrobed fully
- 42 Disrobed partially
- 43 HBD
- 44 UID
- 45 Snatched purse
- 46 Shoplift
- 47 Other

70 INVESTIGATIONS COMPLETED
- 1 Victim Contacted
- 2 Suspect Contacted
- 3 Dusted for Latents / Obtained
- 4 Tool Marks Noted
- 5 Vehicle Shoe Tracks
- 6 Photo/Impressions Taken
- 7 Scene Photographed
- 8 Photos of Victim
- 9 Diagram of Scene
- 10 Neighbors Checked
- 11 Area Checked
- 12 Witnesses Contacted

71 CASE MANAGEMENT
- 1 Suspect Named/Identified/Located
- 2 Suspect Vehicle Identified by Lic No
- 3 Significant/Unique MO
- 4 Limited Number of Suspects
- 5 Identifiable Suspect Vehicle
- 6 Repetitive MO
- 7 Lost Property Traceable
- 8 Useful Prints Obtained
- 9 Other Leads Available for Clearance

ORS 162.375 INITIATING A FALSE REPORT (1) A person commits the crime of initiating a false report if he knowingly initiates a false alarm or report which is transmitted to a fire department, law enforcement agency or other organization that deals with emergencies involving danger to life or property (2) Initiating a false report is a Class C misdemeanor

[ ] I understand that I am liable for all towing and storage costs incurred during the recovery of this vehicle   [ ] Release property/vehicle to _____

The named child is presently (out of my control) (a runaway) and I request that he/she be taken into custody for their own protection

Signature of Person Reporting the Incident _____

72 PHYSICAL FORCE USED BY POLICE Y N	73 INFO BRDCST Y N	74 T/T SENT Y N	75 F/U ASSIGNED TO	76 BY	77 DATE
78 REPORTING OFFICER(S)	79 BPST	80 ASSN	81 SHIFT	82 GRID	APPROVED

COPIES
- [ ] JDC
- [ ] DA
- [ ] Adm
- [ ] Dets
- [ ] News
- [ ] Juv
- [ ] Comm Educ
- [ ] Crime Analys
- [ ] ____

COMPUTER ENTRY
- [ ] Person
- [ ] Veh
- [ ] Crime
- [ ] Prop
- Date ____
- Opr ____

Figure 1-1. Facesheet — Incident Report (Municipal Police)

C.L.A.S.S.
CLACKAMAS COUNTY SHERIFF
2223 S. Kaen Road, Oregon City, OR
CRIME REPORT

DA	JUV	BD	PROP DET	PERS DET	DC	RELATED REPORT
						□ Prop Loss
CR/AN	MAR	EAST	W/N	USF	MCSO	□ PIC □ Custody
						□ Special □ Vehicle
PDP	ME	UDC	OTHER			□ Person □ Other

1 INCIDENT NO

3 CRIME CLASSIFICATION

4 CONNECT NUMBERS/REPORTS

5 DEPUTY ASSIGNED FOLLOW-UP

6 OCCURRED FROM   7 OCCURRED TO   8 REPORTED

9 LOCATION OF OCCURRENCE   10 GRID

VICTIM

11 NAME OF PERSON OR BUSINESS   12 DOB   13 SEX □ Male □ Female   14 RACE

15 RESIDENCE   16 RES PHONE

17 SCHOOL/EMPLOYER/BUS PROPRIETOR   18 OCCUPATION/ POSITION   19 BUS PHONE

20 R/P 21 W 22 NAME   23 DOB   24 SEX □ Male □ Female   25 RACE

26 RESIDENCE   27 RES PHONE   28 BUS PHONE

29 RELATIONSHIP TO VICTIM   30 WITNESS INVOLVEMENT

31 W 32 NAME   33 DOB   34 SEX □ Male □ Female   35 RACE

36 RESIDENCE   37 RES PHONE   38 BUS PHONE

39 RELATIONSHIP TO VICTIM   40 WITNESS INVOLVEMENT

DOCUMENTS

41 DOCUMENT TYPE
□ Personal Check
□ Payroll
□ Bus Check
□ Money Order
□ Credit Card

42 DOCUMENT CLASS
□ NSF
□ Forged
□ Account Closed
□ Stolen
□ Refer To

43 BANK OR SOURCE OF DOCUMENT   44 ACCOUNT NO   45 CHECK INFORMATION

46 ACTION
What part of document written in presence of victim/witness
□ Face □ Endorsement □ Other

47 NAME OF ENDORSER

TARGETS

48 VICTIM
	Sex
1 □ Child	□ M □ F
2 □ Juv	□ M □ F
3 □ Adult	□ M □ F
4 □ Elderly	□ M □ F
5 □ Multiple victims	

49 RESIDENTIAL
1 □ Single Family
2 □ Duplex
3 □ Apt/condo
4 □ Hotel/motel
5 □ Travel trailer
6 □ Mobile home
7 □ Other ____

50 NON RESIDENTIAL
1 □ Open area-private
2 □ Highway/roadway
3 □ Open area-public
4 □ Construction site
5 □ Vehicle
6 □ RV
7 □ Office/prof bldg
8 □ Financial inst
9 □ School
10 □ Drug/medical
11 □ Supermarket/variety
12 □ Convenience store
13 □ Liquor store
14 □ Restaurant
15 □ Fast food
16 □ Tavern/bar
17 □ Gas station
18 □ Indust/mfg
19 □ Warehouse
20 □ Specialty Shop
22 □ Church
23 □ Car Lot
21 □ Other ____

51 TARGETS
1 □ Cash reg/drawer
2 □ Owner/employee
3 □ Safe/cashbox
4 □ Vending machine
5 □ Display items
6 □ Office
7 □ Customer
8 □ Storage/locker
9 □ Other ____

52 PT OF ENTRY/EXIT
	Entry	Exit
1 Unknown	□	□
2 Front	□	□
3 Rear	□	□
4 Side	□	□
5 Grnd level	□	□
6 Upr level	□	□
7 Roof	□	□
8 Door	□	□
9 Sliding glass	□	□
10 Window	□	□
11 Duct/vent	□	□
12 Adjac bldg	□	□
13 Wall	□	□
14 Garage	□	□
15 Trunk/hood	□	□
16 Other	□	□

53 METHOD OF ENTRY EXIT
	Entry	Exit
1 Not successful	□	□
2 No force	□	□
3 Unlocked	□	□
4 Hid/remain in structure	□	□
5 Invited/lawful entry	□	□
6 Forced entry	□	□
7 Bodily force	□	□
8 Pick/slip lock	□	□
9 Cut/break lock	□	□
10 Twist knobs	□	□
11 Saw/drill/burn	□	□
12 Cut glass	□	□
13 Broke Glass	□	□
14 Unique/ extraordinary	□	□
15 Pry Tool	□	□
16 Other ____		

54 SURROUNDING AREA
1 □ Residential
2 □ Business
3 □ Industrial/Mfg
4 □ Recreational
5 □ Institutional
6 □ Other

55 TARGET
1 □ Entire structure
2 □ Basement
3 □ Gar/Carport
4 □ Attic
5 □ Kitchen
6 □ Bedroom
7 □ Family area
8 □ Bathroom
9 □ Storage area
10 □ Other ____

56 TYPE SECURITY
1 □ Alarm
2 □ Bars
3 □ Deadbolt
4 □ Int lights
5 □ Ext lights
6 □ Camera
7 □ Dog
8 □ Operation ID
9 □ Security fence
10 □ Guard
11 □ Prv Sec Pat
12 □ Other

57 MISC ____

SUSPECT ACTIONS

58 SECTION 1
1 □ Mult Suspects
2 □ Used look-out
3 □ Vehicle needed
4 □ Took victims vehicle
5 □ Used stolen vehicle
6 □ Suspect armed
7 □ Discharged weapon
8 □ Smoked
9 □ Ate/drank
10 □ Used matches for light
11 □ Used victim's tools
12 □ Prepared exit
13 □ Defecated
14 □ Turned lights on/off
15 □ Disabled phone
16 □ Shut off power
17 □ Wore mask
18 □ Unique/extraordinary
19 □ Other ____

59 SECTION 2
1 □ Vandalized
2 □ Ransacked
3 □ Knew loc of prop
4 □ Selective in loot
5 □ Took only concealables
6 □ Took prop from vehicle
7 □ Stashed loot
8 □ Shoplift
9 □ Used pillowcase etc
10 □ Other ____

60 SECTION 3
1 □ Inflicted injury
2 □ Threat retaliation
3 □ Forced victim to lay on floor
4 □ Forced victim into vehicle
5 □ Put property in sack/pocket
6 □ Snatched purse
7 □ Offered assist
8 □ Used left hand
9 □ Used right hand
10 □ Took hostage
11 □ Did not speak
12 □ Covered vic face
13 □ Bound/gagged victim
14 □ Demanded specific items
15 □ Other ____

61 SECTION 4
1 □ Knew victim's name
2 □ Molested victim
3 □ Unusual odor
4 □ Masturbated
5 □ Ejaculated
6 □ Unable to erect
7 □ Struck victim
8 □ Made victim disrobe
9 □ Required victim to act
10 □ Raped
11 □ Other sex acts
12 □ Other ____

62 EXACT WORDS OF SUSPECT

63 UNIQUE MO

64 TIME RECEIVED   65 TIME DISPATCHED   66 TIME ARRIVED   67 TIME CLEARED

68 REPORTING OFFICER   69 BPST #   70 AGENCY   71 APPROVED BY

72 REPORTING OFFICER   73 BPST #   74 AGENCY   75 DATA ENTRY

CCP-SF32/1

Figure 1-2. Facesheet — Crime Report (County Sheriff)

1.2 FACESHEET VERSUS NARRATIVE

Police reports generally are divided into two basic areas: the facesheet, sometimes called a coversheet, and the narrative. The facesheet usually has boxes to be checked or filled in. Its primary function is to provide quick access to necessary bits of information common to all cases. This quick access is valuable for crime-reporting purposes, compiling statistics, computer data entry, filing, cross-referencing, and crime-analysis work. The facesheet does not and cannot create the word picture of the event under investigation, nor of the investigation itself. The facesheet is a collection of facts, but has little bearing on what the witnesses add to the case.

Different facesheets typically are used, depending on the specific purpose of the report, e.g., incident reports, crime reports, custody reports, vehicle reports, and worthless document reports. Others include missing person reports, supplemental or follow-up reports, and property reports. Facesheets

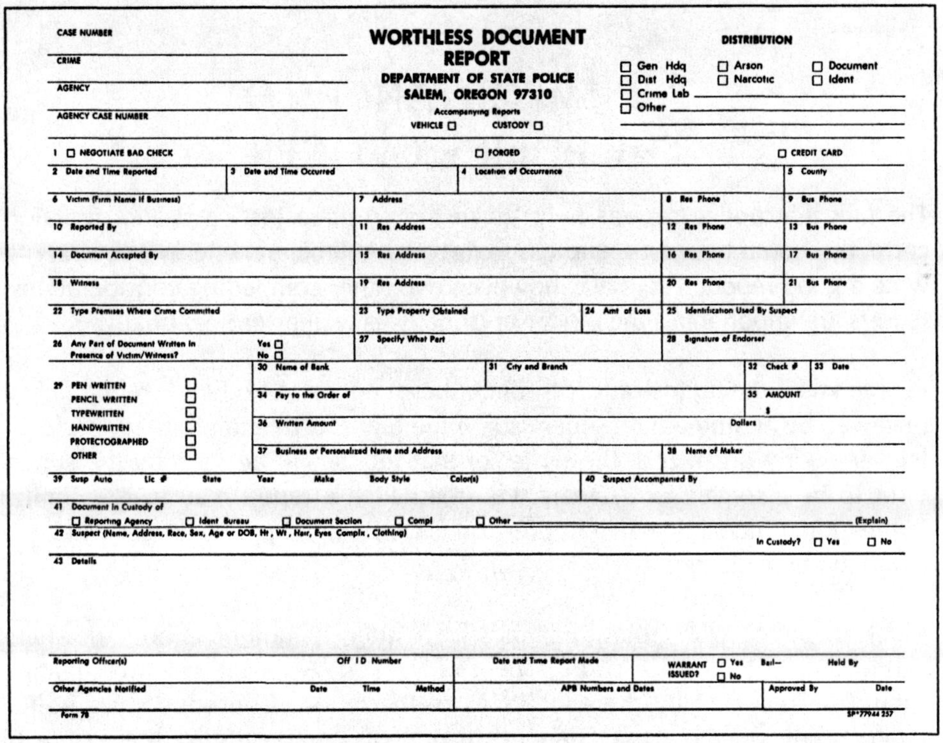
CASE NUMBER
CRIME
AGENCY
AGENCY CASE NUMBER

WORTHLESS DOCUMENT REPORT
DEPARTMENT OF STATE POLICE
SALEM, OREGON 97310
Accompanying Reports
VEHICLE ☐ CUSTODY ☐

DISTRIBUTION
☐ Gen Hdq ☐ Arson ☐ Document
☐ Dist Hdq ☐ Narcotic ☐ Ident
☐ Crime Lab
☐ Other

1 ☐ NEGOTIATE BAD CHECK ☐ FORGED ☐ CREDIT CARD

2 Date and Time Reported | 3 Date and Time Occurred | 4 Location of Occurrence | 5 County
6 Victim (Firm Name If Business) | 7 Address | 8 Res Phone | 9 Bus Phone
10 Reported By | 11 Res Address | 12 Res Phone | 13 Bus Phone
14 Document Accepted By | 15 Res Address | 16 Res Phone | 17 Bus Phone
18 Witness | 19 Res Address | 20 Res Phone | 21 Bus Phone
22 Type Premises Where Crime Committed | 23 Type Property Obtained | 24 Amt of Loss | 25 Identification Used By Suspect
26 Any Part of Document Written In Presence of Victim/Witness? Yes ☐ No ☐ | 27 Specify What Part | 28 Signature of Endorser
29 PEN WRITTEN ☐ PENCIL WRITTEN ☐ TYPEWRITTEN ☐ HANDWRITTEN ☐ PROTECTOGRAPHED ☐ OTHER ☐
30 Name of Bank | 31 City and Branch | 32 Check # | 33 Date
34 Pay to the Order of | 35 AMOUNT $
36 Written Amount | Dollars
37 Business or Personalized Name and Address | 38 Name of Maker
39 Susp Auto Lic # State Year Make Body Style Color(s) | 40 Suspect Accompanied By
41 Document In Custody of ☐ Reporting Agency ☐ Ident Bureau ☐ Document Section ☐ Compl ☐ Other (Explain)
42 Suspect (Name, Address, Race, Sex, Age or DOB, Ht, Wt, Hair, Eyes Complx, Clothing) In Custody? ☐ Yes ☐ No
43 Details

Reporting Officer(s) | Off I D Number | Date and Time Report Made | WARRANT ISSUED? ☐ Yes ☐ No | Bail— | Held By
Other Agencies Notified | Date | Time | Method | APB Numbers and Dates | Approved By | Date
Form 78 SP*77944 257

Figure 1-3. Facesheet — Worthless Document Report (State Police)

have styles that vary not only from report type to report type but from agency to agency, county to county, and state to state. There is little uniformity among facesheet formats. Some stress filling in blanks; others stress checking boxes. While facesheets serve valuable functions, they must be accompanied by a narrative if there is any investigative activity that led to the report being written.

See Figures 1-1, 1-2, and 1-3 for examples of typical facesheets.

After the facesheet the narrative section contains the entire police investigative effort written in sentence and paragraph format. Readers rely on the narrative section to understand how the information accumulated during the investigation shows which crime was committed and who committed it. It is this section that enables readers to evaluate the case for its strengths and weaknesses. It is this section that must concentrate on witnesses.

Improving the writing of the narrative section is the goal of this text.

1.3 IMPORTANCE TO THE POLICE OFFICER

The fact that police reports help make the criminal justice system function correctly should be reason enough to devote the time and energy necessary to write a good report. There are, however, two other compelling considerations: reports are important to the officer personally as well as professionally.

People know the police officer through these reports. An officer's report is first reviewed by an immediate supervisor. If the report is difficult to read, misleading, or poorly organized, the writer of that report will be seen by the supervisor to be disorganized. Others who read such a report may gain a similar impression. Once a negative impression is created, the police officer will have a difficult time changing it.

Much of police work today depends on written communication. An officer cannot afford to overlook this aspect of the job. An excellent investigation should be reflected by the excellence of the report. Consequently a police officer's advancement may depend in part on demonstrating the ability to communicate high-quality work through well-written reports.

A police officer may testify in court as to the findings and observations in a particular investigation. Lawyers will ask questions based not only on what the officer says on the witness stand but also on what the officer wrote in the report. If the report is unclear, ambiguous, or inaccurate, the cross-examination is likely to be lengthy and vigorous. The same is true if the report is disorganized and hard to read.

A police officer may refer to the report for the purpose of refreshing memory while testifying. If the report is clear, easy to read, and organized, the officer is likely to find that (1) cross-examination will be short and to the point, and (2) facts can be recalled more easily and testified to with confidence.

A police officer who has left out certain facts or information from the report may be embarrassed on the witness stand. The defense attorney can argue effectively that if something is not written down in the report, it either did not happen or was insignificant because a police officer is trained to report important, relevant observations during an investigation.

1.4 IMPORTANCE TO SOCIETY

Not only are police reports necessary to the proper functioning of the criminal justice system and valuable to the ones who write the reports, they are important to society as a whole. Much of the work police officers do has high-visibility results, especially the investigation of criminal activity and the arrest and prosecution of those who commit crimes. Criminal cases are often media news items and common topics of popular discussion. It is important to society that otherwise good cases not be damaged by poorly written reports. The public's confidence in its law enforcement agencies should always remain high. The public trust rests with the investigating officers' professionalism and competence.

Good investigations and well-written reports have a positive and beneficial effect on the victims of crime and on the private citizens who will later appear as witnesses in court. These people the laws were designed to protect and serve are often the last ones given consideration by the criminal justice system. These people deserve the best efforts of those who work in the system.

SUMMARY

Police reports are the single link between the police officer's field investigation and the ability of others to understand and to use the results of that investigation. The report must be written to satisfy all types of readers who use reports to make decisions. These decisions generally impact others. But the greatest impact a police report can have on society as a whole is as a source of accurate information in the prosecution of criminals. A good police report has far-reaching consequences, particularly in helping prosecutors make the correct charging decisions and in gaining convictions.

Police reports usually contain a facesheet and a narrative. The facesheet contains basic facts that must be collected regardless of the crime, such as dates, times, and names and addresses of victims and witnesses.

The narrative section, on the other hand, is needed to give the reader a word picture of the investigation. It also serves as a means by which the officer's memory can be refreshed prior to testifying.

Well-written narrative police reports are the lifeblood of a healthy criminal justice system. They carry valuable information to every component, thus enabling people in the system to do their various jobs accurately and efficiently.

▼ REVIEW QUESTIONS

1. Explain how the narrative police report is important to
   a) the report writer
   b) the police agency
   c) the prosecutor
2. What are the differences between the functions of a facesheet and a narrative report?

CHAPTER TWO

▼

What Makes a Good Report

2.1 DISTINGUISHING FACTS VERSUS WITNESSES

In the dark early morning stillness of August 26, 1974, in the community of Rural Dell, Lester Roark, a somewhat drunk 42-year-old handyman, crept into the house of Crystal Parker, an 81-year-old retired bookkeeper who lived alone. Lester was looking for money to steal. Despite his efforts to be quiet, he bumped into furniture and walls. The noise awakened Crystal. She walked into her darkened hallway where she was confronted by Lester who had armed himself with a garden hoe he had found by the back door. Crystal began to scream, and Lester struck her repeatedly with the hoe until she stopped moving. He found a can of gasoline in the garage and splashed it all around, including on Crystal's body. He ignited the gasoline and ran from the house. No one saw him leave.

Crystal's body was found at about 9:30 A.M. in the still-smoldering ashes of her house. An autopsy conducted later that afternoon showed she had been hacked to death with the garden hoe found embedded in her neck. The brutal murder-arson shocked the community and stymied local law enforcement. Some people in the community of Rural Dell speculated that Lester may have committed the murder. In fact Lester was questioned several times by the police but consistently denied knowing anything about the crime. For several months the police investigation made little progress.

In mid-December, Warren Lucksinger, a field representative for a machine tool company, telephoned the Rural Dell Police Department. He told them that he had just read about the case. He lived in another state and only visited Rural Dell twice a year. He was last in Rural Dell on August 26, 1974, at a cafe not far from Crystal Parker's house. It was about sunrise. He was just finishing his breakfast before leaving town when a man sat down at his table. From the man's disheveled appearance, slurred speech, and poor coordination he thought the man had been drinking. The man seemed to be about 45 years old and in need of a shave and a haircut. The man did not make a scene but quietly rambled on to himself about being in trouble because he had hurt a nice old lady with a hoe. The man also mumbled something about burning down a house. Mr. Lucksinger thought the man was hallucinating so he quickly paid his bill and left. As he passed the man, Mr. Lucksinger smelled an odor of gasoline about him.

With Mr. Lucksinger's information the local police picked up Lester Roark and questioned him again. During questioning, Lester confessed to killing Crystal and burning down her house. He was arrested and charged with the crime.

Prior to trial, Lester's lawyer was successful in having the judge suppress the evidence of Lester's confession to the police. The only remaining evidence of Lester's involvement in the crime was the testimony of Warren Lucksinger.

Three days before Lester's trial, Warren Lucksinger was killed in a single-car accident when his car left the road on a dangerous mountain curve during a rainstorm.

The case against Lester Roark was dismissed and he was released from jail. Although everyone knew he committed the crime, he was never convicted because there was no way to prove it. The facts of the crime never changed: Crystal was murdered; her house was burned down; Lester was the one who did it. The only change in the case was that there was now no way to prove that Lester was the murderer. That proof was lost with the death of the witness, Warren Lucksinger.

The relationship between the facts of a case and witnesses is clear: without witnesses there are no facts as far as the prosecution of a criminal case is concerned.

2.2 INVESTIGATIVE GOALS VERSUS REPORT WRITING GOALS

There are significant differences between the investigative function and the report writing function. The most important differences, however, lie not in the relative natures of the activities nor the skills and knowledge required for each, but in their goals. An appreciation of the differences between the investigative goal and the report writing goal is necessary for a complete understanding of the report writing method explained in this text.

The police officer's principal investigative goals are to learn what happened (i.e., what crime was committed: theft or robbery? assault or self-defense?) and to determine who committed the crime. To accomplish these goals, the officer looks beyond people who have heard rumors and indulge in speculation and seeks out those people who have firsthand knowledge about the facts. These people are called *witnesses*. In a successful investigation the officer would talk to enough witnesses to become satisfied as to what crime was committed and who committed it.

In the case of the murder of Crystal Parker some of the citizens of Rural Dell speculated that Lester Roark was responsible for the murder, but until Warren Lucksinger came forward, there was no way to prove that Lester was guilty. After having interviewed Warren Lucksinger, the investigating officer was convinced of Lester Roark's guilt even before Lester confessed. The investigative goal of determining who murdered Crystal and set fire to her house was accomplished.

An investigating officer will eventually write a police report to explain what was learned during the investigation. If the officer's report is limited to the same goals as the investigation, that is, to explain what crime was committed and who committed it, the report will not provide the necessary information needed for the criminal justice system. This is because the report concentrated on reporting facts and ignored how those facts were going to be established at trial. It ignored witnesses.

If the officer who interviewed Warren Lucksinger simply wrote in the narrative report that the investigation had progressed to the point that it was established with some certainty that Lester Roark was the murderer, that report would be inadequate. The officer must instead report what Mr. Lucksinger said during the interview so that whoever read that report would come to the same conclusion as did the officer—Lester did it.

The goal of the investigation is to learn facts, but only through firsthand witnesses. The goal of the narrative report, however, is to write about what these firsthand witnesses saw and heard so that the reader can draw accurate conclusions about what the facts are and how they can be established at trial.

2.3 LINKING FACTS WITH WITNESS CREDIBILITY

A narrative police report must focus on witnesses. With very few exceptions, no fact can be presented in court except through the testimony of a witness under oath on the witness stand who testifies from firsthand knowledge. This very important maxim comes from several constitutional and statutory laws that guarantee that defendants in criminal cases have the right to confront in court every witness against them. Facts, in a very real and practical sense, are of less importance than witnesses.

Facts are obviously important during the investigation of a case and also during the trial of the case. Officers seek answers to the questions What happened? and Who did it? during the investigation. Prosecutors read police reports to learn what crime was committed and who was responsible. While there is a keen interest in facts, the ultimate question is always Can the facts be proven in court? Part of the answer to this question is knowing who the witnesses are and getting them on the witness stand at the trial of the case.

But more is involved than just getting a witness on the witness stand and asking questions of that witness. The credibility of the witness is also important.

Witnesses testify under oath. The jury — or the judge, if there is no jury — decides what the facts are, based on whether or not they find the witnesses credible. The jury (or judge) must also believe the witnesses in order to determine what the facts are. Defense attorneys exploit every opportunity to attack the credibility of the witnesses for the prosecution. Some witnesses have inherent credibility problems because they are biased, have criminal convictions, or have reputations for being untruthful.

A narrative report writer can create credibility problems for witnesses by writing the narrative report in a way that concentrates on reporting facts and ignores the reality that witnesses are necessary to prove those facts. For example, an officer may learn that the getaway car was a light blue, late-1970s, Chevrolet four door and had a partial plate of JDE 7—. June Getts saw the car only from the side and gave the physical description. Her 10-year-old son, Thomas Getts, was the one who actually saw the plate and told the officer about the plate description after the officer had interviewed Thomas's mother.

A narrative report that lists June Getts as the only witness and omits any mention of Thomas will be inaccurate. Thomas Getts, not having been identified as a witness in the report, will likely not be subpoenaed to the trial. Moreover the inaccurate report is also likely to cause problems for June Getts when she testifies. At the trial, June Getts's testimony that she never saw the license plate will be at odds with the narrative report that implies that she was the source of that information. Unless the officer has an independent recollection that the license plate information came from Thomas Getts, the officer may conclude from the report that June Getts saw the license plate. That officer is very likely to testify that the license plate information must have come from June Getts, thus undermining her testimony and allowing the defense attorney to attack her credibility.

A narrative report that concentrates on reporting facts and does not focus on reporting about witnesses will always run the risk of creating credibility problems at trial.

2.4 EASY TO READ

A good report is one that is easy to read. A police report is written to be read. Anything that can be done to make it easier to read will be worth the effort. The police report's narrative section must be attractive and inviting to the reader, leading the reader logically from the beginning to the end. It must allow the reader to locate specific information quickly without having to read or reread the entire report.

The officer who writes the report becomes a reader when months later that same officer is called to the witness stand to be asked questions about the investigation. The officer will read the report prior to testifying and is likely to read it again while on the stand. Just because the officer wrote the report is no guarantee that the facts will later be remembered without the report being reviewed. The need to get to specific information quickly makes a highly-readable report very beneficial to a police officer testifying on the witness stand.

2.5 EASY TO WRITE

A good report is one that is easy to write. It must allow an officer to get through the actual writing process comfortably. Officers will be able to learn a method more quickly and with less effort if all narratives can be written using the same method and the same rules, regardless of either the type of crime or the type of investigation.

The method of report writing explained in this text allows all narrative reports to be written using the same format and the same rules, regardless of the crime involved or the nature of the investigation.

Police officers write a lot of reports, so they have many opportunities to practice good report writing methods. Once good habits are formed, the reports become easier to write and more professional in appearance and content.

2.6 ORGANIZING THE NARRATIVE

A good narrative report must be organized. The narrative format described in this text is arranged in the form of an outline. There are six sections to this outline: <u>SUMMARY</u>, <u>MENTIONED</u>, <u>ACTION TAKEN</u>, <u>STATEMENTS</u>, <u>EVIDENCE</u>, and <u>ACTION RECOMMENDED</u>. Chapter 3 explains the format for the six-section narrative. It also includes rules for writing paragraphs, as well as the proper use of headings, capitalizations, underlinings, margins, indentations, spacing, and columns. The rules for writing each of the six sections are covered in detail in chapter 4. Chapter 5 contains practical suggestions concerning words, language, and grammar for clear, objective, and effective writing.

SUMMARY

The officer's field investigation is an exercise in collecting facts about what crime was committed and who committed it. Officers are trained to deal in firsthand information, not rumor or suspicion. Therefore officers routinely seek out witnesses who have such firsthand information. The police report, especially the narrative section, is the place where the officer describes the field investigation results in such a way that others can use those results. These people rely on the narrative report for an explanation of the facts in the same way the officer learned those facts. They need to know who the witnesses are and what each had to say regarding firsthand knowledge of the facts.

Police reports that simply recite facts without conveying the exact source(s) of those facts are poorly written reports. Witnesses are the very foundation of any investigation. Therefore any good narrative police report must concentrate on witnesses, not just on facts.

A good narrative police report, like any other written document, needs to lead the reader logically from beginning to end. The information should not only be clear but also easy to find without having to reread the entire report. The six-section format was created specifically to cause the police officer to write about witnesses and not just report facts.

▼ REVIEW QUESTIONS

1. Explain in your own words the meaning of the phrase "witnesses are more important than facts." Give an example that illustrates the meaning of the phrase.
2. Explain how a report writer becomes a report reader.
3. Contrast the goals of a police investigation with the goals of a narrative report.
4. What is the connection between the credibility of witnesses and the ability to prove facts in court?

▼

CHAPTER THREE

The Narrative Format Explained

3.1 THE SIX MAJOR SECTIONS

The narrative portion of the police report is divided into six sections: SUMMARY, MENTIONED, ACTION TAKEN, STATEMENTS, EVIDENCE, and ACTION RECOMMENDED. Each of these sections will be examined in turn for appropriate content and style of presentation.

The major reason the narrative is divided into these particular sections is to help the officer write about the two most important objectives: the identification of witnesses, and a clear statement as to what the witnesses can be expected to testify to when called upon in court.

There are additional reasons for dividing the narrative report into these six sections. There is a need for uniformity in teaching about writing the narrative. The method urged in this text allows every report to be written the same way, regardless of the subject matter of the investigation or the type of investigative activity conducted. This is not only helpful to instructors, it is also one of the major reasons police officers can adapt to this method and become successful report writers in a short time.

Another important reason for using these six sections in the narrative is because they make the report easy to read. By having distinct sections, each containing a different type of information, a reader can skip to particular areas in the report to find specific information without having to skim the entire report. The report writer becomes a report reader upon being subpoenaed to court to testify about the facts of the investigation. With report in hand, the officer takes the witness stand to answer questions either from memory or from memory refreshed by the report. It is important to the officer's confidence and credibility that the information be easily and quickly found in the report. Seconds can seem like minutes if the officer must scan several pages of the narrative report in order to be able to answer a question on the witness stand.

Dividing the narrative report into sections, each with its own type of information and individual format, not only makes the report easy to read, it makes the writer appear very organized and competent. The six sections of the narrative will contain all the information necessary to understand and evaluate the strengths and weaknesses of the case under investigation.

Of the six sections, four make up the core of the narrative report and deal exclusively with correctly reporting information about witnesses. These four are <u>MENTIONED</u>, <u>ACTION TAKEN</u>, <u>STATEMENTS</u>, and <u>EVIDENCE</u>. The format these sections will follow is explained later in this chapter.

The remaining two sections, <u>SUMMARY</u> and <u>ACTION RECOMMENDED</u>, begin and end the narrative report, but do not deal directly with witnesses. They are important to the reader in other ways. <u>SUMMARY</u> introduces the reader to the subject matter of the report. This becomes important in cases where there are multiple reports covering the same criminal investigation. This makes it easier to locate a particular report from among others. <u>ACTION RECOMMENDED</u>, the concluding few lines in the narrative, allows the writer of the report to express an opinion as to what the next investigative efforts in the case should be.

Each section will always follow its own format. In addition the content of each of the six sections will be written according to the same rules from one report to the next. (These rules will be explained in more detail in chapter 4.) The fact that the format remains consistent from one report to the next should make it easier for an officer to adjust to the method described in this text.

SUMMARY: A few lines of writing; gives a brief overview of what will be contained in the body of the narrative report.

MENTIONED: A list of people; lists all suspects and witnesses, with a very brief description of how each is involved in the case. If necessary, information for locating a particular person in the future is also included.

ACTION TAKEN: Written in paragraph form; statement by the investigating officer writing the report, explaining what was done from beginning to end in the investigative period covered by this report; explains the reasons for actions taken, so as to make the report understandable and/or to satisfy stop/frisk/search/seizure laws.

STATEMENTS: Written in paragraph form; contains statements from each person interviewed by the officer. The significance and contribution of each witness is evaluated from the statements given here.

EVIDENCE: A list of things; lists all physical evidence either recovered (e.g., stolen property) or generated (e.g., photographs) in the investigative period covered by the report. This section is written in a four-column format, the headings being: ITEM, LOCATION, SEIZED BY, and DISPOSITION.

ACTION RECOMMENDED: A few lines of writing; writer's recommendation(s) about what further investigative activity, if any, remains to be undertaken.

Figure 3-1. Overview of the six-section format for police reports

An overview of the format is briefly described in Figure 3-1.

In the narrative report the section headings will always be written regardless of whether or not any information will be written under them. In cases where there is nothing to be written, the officer should write the particular section heading and then "None" under it. For example, if no physical evidence is collected, the EVIDENCE section will appear as shown in Figure 3-2.

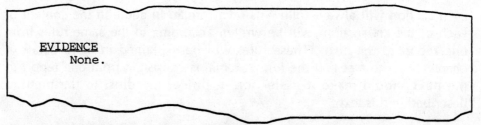

```
EVIDENCE
    None.
```

Figure 3-2. How to indicate "nothing to report" under a report heading

3.2 MARGINS

Each major section heading should be capitalized and underlined. The heading should also be written on one line on the left side of the page with nothing else written on that line. All six section headings should be written at the same margin line on the left side of the page. All of the writing under each major section heading should be indented one-half inch from the left margin, as in Figure 3-3.

3.3 SENTENCES

Sentences should be short, simple, and direct because the longer the sentence is, the more difficult it is for the reader to follow it, and that lends confusion to your report, whereas short sentences lend emphasis, clarity, and communication, which is what any good report writer strives for, which is what this text is all about, and as an example, this entire paragraph is one sentence with no periods, and at this point, you should feel as though you are smothering in words and wish there would be a period so you could take a breath.

On the other hand, short sentences are easy to read. They allow for much needed breathing spaces. Short sentences also provide a refreshing directness seldom found in longer sentences.

```
SUMMARY
    On April 7, 19—, at about 4:30 A.M. the home of
Arlene Raye Simpson at 16345 Highway 12A, Mist, was
burglarized. Michael John Burnam was arrested.
```

Figure 3-3. Margins to be observed in writing a police report

3.4 PARAGRAPHS

Block Form

All paragraphs should be written in a block paragraph form, as in Figure 3-4. Do not indent the first line of the paragraph. Observe the half-inch margin for every line. The writer distinguishes one paragraph from another by leaving a blank line between them, giving the written page the appearance of having breathing spaces between paragraphs.

Length

Paragraphs, like sentences, should not be too long. Paragraphs that are more than a couple of inches in length may make it harder for the reader to follow the train of thought. Just as shorter sentences allow for much needed breathing spaces, shorter paragraphs allow the reader a chance to pause and digest what was just read before continuing on.

See Figure 3-5 for an example of a paragraph that is hard to read.

Having some variety in the length of paragraphs not only gives the reader a break, it adds to the attractiveness of the narrative. Varying the length of the

```
I saw Mr. Moore lying on the sidewalk on his
back. He seemed to be in pain because he was
clutching his stomach and groaning as he twisted
from one side to the other. There were several
people standing by, watching Mr. Moore.

I walked over to my patrol car, called the
dispatcher, and asked him to send an ambulance. I
walked back to where Mr. Moore was and saw that
he had become unconscious in the minute or two
that I had been gone. A young man, Mr. Gibson,
stepped forward and began to give Mr. Moore
mouth-to-mouth resuscitation.

A bystander, Mrs. Lindquist, told me that she had
seen Mr. Moore fighting with a large man with a
red beard and an eyepatch just before Mr. Moore
collapsed on the sidewalk. She told me that she
thought she saw the large man stab Mr. Moore in
the stomach with an ice pick just before he fell.
```

Figure 3-4. Block paragraph form

paragraphs should not be carried to an extreme. Most paragraphs should still
be a couple of inches in length.

SIR: On August 23, 19——, I recovered two stolen
VW sedans in a secluded field at the dead-end of
S.W. Panner Road. These vehicles were both
reported stolen to the Greenfield Police
Department, their case numbers 690241 and
690237. At 9:30 A.M. dispatch requested that I
call Mr. Palaunk at 225-0247. He said he saw two
young males in the VWs that I'd just recovered.
He said he thought that one of the young males
lived at 14177 S.W. Panner Road. Sgt. Weitz and
I went to that address which was at the end of a
long driveway in a secluded area approximately
one-half mile east of where I had just recovered
the two VWs. Upon arrival at this address, I saw
a VW engine and VW transaxle sitting in plain
view next to a barn. I went to the house and
knocked at the front door. A young girl answered
the door. She identified herself as Bonnie Ruth
Rizor. She said she knew nothing about the VW
engine or parts. She said that her brother,
Jimmie Rizor, was asleep in bed and the VW parts
were his. She agreed to wake him up, and a few
minutes later Jimmie Rizor came to the door. He
told me at first that he bought the VW engine
and transaxle from a friend, "Jeremy," (last
name unknown) for $125.00. He said he bought
them several days ago. He said he lived at the
residence and agreed to walk out to the barn
with me. He said that we could go into the barn.
Before entering the barn he said that there was
a Honda motorcycle in the barn and that it was
his. We went into the barn and I ran the VIN on
the motorcycle and dispatch told me that it had
been reported stolen to the Greenfield Police
Department, their case number 686222. I
immediately read Mr. Rizor his Miranda rights at
9:45 A.M. He said he understood them. He told me
that he got the Honda motorcycle from an old man
at a garage sale. He said he'd traded his Honda
125 for it. He said he had no idea who the man

Figure 3-5. Example of a hard to read paragraph

```
At 10:53 P.M. I saw a 1983 Plymouth drive slowly
westbound on Fourth Street and then turn north
on Alder. The driver was alone in the car and
had almost slowed down to a stop as he turned
onto Alder. I was able to get a good look at his
face at that point, since there was a
streetlight illuminating the area. He parked
next to the crosswalk at Fifth Street, got out,
and walked directly to the billboard at the
southeast corner of Fifth and Alder.

He stooped down and quickly picked up the
briefcase.

The man ran back to the 1983 Plymouth and looked
in all directions. He then threw the briefcase
onto the front seat and got in. I radioed to the
other deputies in unmarked surveillance cars who
were assigned to follow anyone who picked up the
ransom to tell them that the ransom had been
picked up.
```

Figure 3-6. Typical paragraph lengths

On occasion when the writer wants to emphasize a particular fact or statement, it should be isolated into a one-sentence paragraph. One-sentence paragraphs in the midst of larger paragraphs stand out from the larger paragraphs, as in Figure 3-6. Because the reader's attention is drawn to things that stand out, the reader's attention is also drawn to the fact or thought expressed in that one-sentence paragraph.

```
STATEMENTS
    JOSEPH MARTIN GIERLICH told me that he was Mr.
Kruger's brother-in-law and a good friend of
his. He said that at about 3:30 or 4:00 P.M. he
returned home from Aumsville where he had been
golfing and parked his car in his driveway
about three feet from the garage door.
```

Figure 3-7. The format to follow for reporting a witness's statement

3.5 THE FORMAT FOR STATEMENTS

The format to be used when writing witnesses' statements under the major section heading <u>STATEMENTS</u> is shown in Figure 3-7. Capitalize and underline the witness's name and then write the words "told me" after the name. Next write a few lines explaining who the witness is and how this witness is related to the case. Finally, write the witness's statement.

However, the format to be used when writing a suspect's statement under the major section heading <u>STATEMENTS</u> is quite different. The suspect's name must be capitalized and underlined and the word "suspect" written after the name. Then write "I interviewed [title + last name] on . . ." followed by the date, time, and place of the interview, along with the names of the people who were present during the interview. Next include information about the Miranda rights and responses (or information about why the circumstances were not custodial).

After that first paragraph begin the second paragraph of the suspect's statement by writing "[title + last name] told me . . ." See Figure 3-8.

<u>STATEMENTS</u>
    <u>JENNIFER JILL SCHEER</u>, suspect. I interviewed Mrs. Scheer at 1:25 A.M. on March 17, 19——, in the garage of Mrs. Kruse's home. We were alone. I first read Mrs. Scheer her Miranda rights from a card. I asked her if she understood her rights and she said, "Of course."

    Mrs. Scheer told me that she didn't think she'd had too much to drink but was unable to remember things too clearly. I asked her how much she'd had to drink and she said, "I must have had too much or I wouldn't have done that to that guy. I'm sorry."

Figure 3-8. The format to follow for reporting a suspect's statement

3.6 THE FORMAT FOR EVIDENCE

The only place in the narrative where the writing is done in columns is under the major section heading <u>EVIDENCE</u>, as in Figure 3-9. This section is written using a four-column format. The columns are labeled and written in the following order: <u>ITEM</u>, <u>LOCATION</u>, <u>SEIZED BY</u>, <u>DISPOSITION</u>. The first column is indented one-half inch to the right of the beginning of the section heading <u>EVIDENCE</u>. Each of the items of evidence is listed under <u>ITEM</u>. Specific information about each item is written under the next three column headings.

Of principal importance under the <u>SEIZED BY</u> column is the reporting of the name(s) of the person(s) who can identify the evidence. This is the person, for example, who actually recovered the physical evidence, or who took or can testify about the photographs, or who read the Miranda rights card.

There are several reasons why evidence should be reported in this manner.

1. The report looks better and is easier to read at a glance, making the writer look very organized and professional.
2. It forces the writer to write about each of the four essential areas that the reader must know about in order to understand the relevance of the evidence.

```
EVIDENCE
     ITEM          LOCATION      SEIZED BY     DISPOSITION
     21" Sony      Mr. Adams's   Mr. Adams     Returned to
     color TV      front room    and myself    Mr. Adams

     diagram       Cave          myself        PIC 001762,
     statement     Junction                    item 8
     by Mrs.       Police Dept.
     Geiber

     strike        Mr. Adams's   myself        same,
     plate         rear door                   item 3
```

Figure 3-9. The format to follow for the <u>EVIDENCE</u> section

3. It may improve evidence-gathering techniques. An investigating officer will be more likely to obtain the necessary information for each item seized during the investigation if the officer knows that the information will have to be included under one of the columns of the EVIDENCE section.

SUMMARY

The six-section format for the narrative police report is very much like an outline. It guides the police officer through the writing of narrative reports. Each section is written with a distinct purpose, but all are written with the idea that witnesses are more important to a police report than is a mere collection of facts. The format for the narrative weaves the use of margins, capitalizations, underlinings, spacing, and columns into a crisp pattern that makes the writing and the reading of the report easier.

The sameness of the format from one narrative report to the next satisfies two needs: the need for uniformity in teaching, and the need for uniformity in the report review process. Officers need to learn quickly the correct method of writing narrative police reports because of the high volume of reports they write. Supervisors need to be able to review narrative reports quickly to evaluate the officer's case and performance.

A narrative report that uses the six-section format and concentrates on witnesses is a strong report. It fulfills the need of the criminal justice system for an unbreakable link between law enforcement and prosecution.

▼ REVIEW QUESTIONS

1. Give four reasons for dividing the narrative report into six sections.
2. Explain how each of the four core sections of the narrative report forces the officer to write about witnesses instead of facts.
3. How does the format for witnesses' statements differ from the format for suspects' statements?

▼ WRITING DRILLS

1. Rewrite the following paragraph using block form paragraphs, proper paragraph length, and emphasis of a particular fact by means of a one-sentence paragraph.

    On November 11, 19—, at 4:10 P.M. Deputy Callas searched Mrs. Graybill and her vehicle to make sure she had no money or drugs. I gave Mrs. Graybill $200.00 in Special Investigation Unit funds as follows: one $50.00 bill (SN 182734243A), one $50.00 bill (SN C21648221A), and one $100.00 bill (SN F68150624A). Mrs. Graybill then drove her car to Mr. Willmore's house at 15631 Roselli Avenue. I watched Mrs. Graybill the entire time. I saw her enter Mr. Willmore's house at 4:15 P.M. At 4:20 P.M. Mr. Willmore left his house and drove a cream-colored car to a house on the southwest corner of Calaroga Street and Moss Hill Road just outside of Nyssa. I followed Mr. Willmore in a surveillance vehicle, leaving Deputy Larossa behind to watch Mr. Willmore's house. Mr. Willmore went into the house at Calaroga and Moss Hill Road at 4:26 P.M. and left the house at 4:31 P.M. with an adult male who was approximately 30 years of age, 5'9", and 190 lbs. He had black hair tied with a red bandanna, a full dark beard, black leatherlike jacket, blue jeans, and dark boots. They stood in the driveway and talked. At 4:40 P.M. Mr. Willmore got in his car and left, and the bearded man returned to the house. I followed Mr. Willmore back to his house. He got back at 4:48 P.M. and went inside. At 4:52 P.M. Mrs. Graybill left the house, got into her car, and drove to the Carlyle Landing Strip, with me following. Deputy Callas again searched Mrs. Graybill and her car and found no money but did find a small plastic baggie containing suspected cocaine in her right front jacket pocket. Mrs. Graybill said she bought it from Mr. Willmore for $200.00.

2. Using only the important facts from the following information, write a proper beginning for a witness statement in the STATEMENTS section.

    You interviewed Maxine Noel Koopman, who was a witness to an assault. She was an 82-year-old widow whose husband had been a retired home appliance salesman. She happened to be in the City Center Mall parking lot at 2:30 P.M. on August 6, 19—, on her way to the Shoppers' Bazaar, a department store where she was planning to buy her daughter-in-law a birthday present. She parked her 1991 Chevrolet Caprice and was on her way to the store when she saw a young man kicking at another person who was on the ground curled into a ball and moaning and crying as if in pain.

3. Using only the important facts from the following information, write a proper beginning paragraph for a suspect interview in the STATEMENTS section.

    You interviewed Dwight Hales, a suspect in an embezzlement case you were investigating. The interview took place in the employees' lunchroom of Gile's Menswear Store, 4746 South Monroe Street, Baxterville, at 6:30 P.M. on July 14, 19—. Before interviewing him, you advised him of his Miranda rights. When you asked if he understood them, he said, "Yes, I understand them."

4. Using only the important facts from the following information, write a proper EVIDENCE section.

    You investigated an assault that took place in the Phillip Sacket residence at 227 Boulder Avenue, Reedsport. You were handed a tire iron by Deputy Lober, who told you he found it in the bushes next to the front porch of the Sackett residence. Your investigation revealed that this tire iron was the probable weapon used in the assault. You expect to send it to the crime lab to be processed for trace evidence such as blood and hair. You also expect to process it for latent prints. Another piece of evidence, a Greyhound bus ticket, was given to you by Mrs. Sackett, who told you that she found it on the front floorboard of a 1969 Bronco parked in the Sackett driveway.

▼ NOTES

CHAPTER FOUR

▼

Rules for Writing Each Section

4.1 <u>SUMMARY</u>

The first section of the narrative police report is <u>SUMMARY</u>. <u>SUMMARY</u> explains what the narrative report is all about. The essential facts are stated in one location so that anyone interested in only those facts need look no further. For example, a person scanning several reports for a particular one needs to look at only the <u>SUMMARY</u> sections.

The narrative portion of all police reports (e.g., original crime report, supplemental report, person report, etc.) should contain a <u>SUMMARY</u> section.

The <u>SUMMARY</u> should be brief: two or three lines are usually sufficient. No mention should be made of what the officer did, nor should any details of the investigation itself be written under <u>SUMMARY</u>. It should begin with the word "On," followed by the date, time, and location of the significant event, plus a brief description of that event. If the exact date or time of the significant event is not known, then the <u>SUMMARY</u> will begin with "Between," followed by the dates and/or times and the location of the significant event, plus a brief description of that event. The significant event to be described in the <u>SUMMARY</u> is the event that prompted the investigative activity and led to the narrative report being written. Obviously, every report will have a different significant event described in the <u>SUMMARY</u>, depending on what is being investigated.

EXAMPLE #1 (Named person arrested)

```
SUMMARY
     On June 22, 19—, between 11:30 A.M. and 4:45
     P.M. the residence of Michael Thomas Nyhoff at
     141 W. Lee Drive, Netarts, was burglarized.
     Patrick William Stout was arrested.
```

EXAMPLE #2 (Suspect identified)

```
SUMMARY·
     On May 16, 19—, at about 7:35 P.M. Sandra Jane
     Powell was forcibly raped in the public parking
     garage at 1818 Taylor Street, Dillard, and a
     suspect was identified.
```

EXAMPLE #3 (No suspect)

```
SUMMARY
     On March 21, 19—, between 7:00 P.M. and 11:30
     P.M. a lawn mower was stolen from Mark Andrew
     Jacobson's garage at 1008 Maxam Road, Shaniko.
```

Figure 4-1. Examples of SUMMARY in original crime reports

There are two types of SUMMARY sections. One is the SUMMARY for an original crime report. It will contain the date, time, and place of the crime, along with a brief description of the crime, because the crime is the significant event that prompted the investigation. The last part of this type of SUMMARY will: (a) explain that a named person was arrested, (b) indicate that a suspect was identified, or (c) say nothing in the event there is no suspect.

Three examples of an original crime report SUMMARY are illustrated in Figure 4-1.

The second type of SUMMARY concerns an investigative report about events that happened after the original crime report was written. This type of SUMMARY begins with the word "On" and is followed by the date, time, and place of the significant event that led to the report being written, plus a very

```
SUMMARY
     On August 23, 19—, at 8:30 A.M. Dennis Martin
     Rasmussen was interviewed at his work place,
     Vista Floor Coverings, 2828 N. Balcomb Street,
     Wemme, concerning his knowledge of the burglary
     of the Quintero residence.
```

Figure 4-2. Example of SUMMARY in follow-up report

brief description of that event. For example, in the case of a burglary of Mr. Quintero's house on August 15, 19—, assume that eight days after the burglary, a police officer interviewed a witness, Mr. Rasmussen, at his place of work concerning what he knew of the burglary.

In this case, the SUMMARY for the officer's report of that interview would appear as shown in Figure 4-2.

4.2 MENTIONED

All people whose names came up during the portion of the investigation that led to the report being written should be listed under MENTIONED. These include victims, witnesses, and suspects. Officers from other agencies who assisted in the investigation should also be named under MENTIONED; however, officers from the same agency as the officer writing the report need not be listed. The names listed under MENTIONED should be capitalized, underlined, and indented one-half inch to the right of the beginning of the MENTIONED section heading. Leave a blank line between each name.

Following each name should be a word or phrase describing the person's status in the case (e.g., victim, eyewitness, suspect's roommate, suspect, emergency room nurse).

If the information on the facesheet is insufficient to locate a particular person in the future, additional information about how to locate that person should be

```
MENTIONED
    ERNEST LESLIE HASKINS, victim.

    SARAH EMILY PROUTY, witness, will soon be moving
    to Colorado to go to school at Colorado A & M,
    but can be reached by calling her mother, Clara
    J. Prouty, (503) 871-3232, 414 Harrison St., La
    Pine, Oregon.

    JESSE HENRY HEMLESCH, witness.

    NANCY ELAINE PROBST, witness.

    UNIDENTIFIED, suspect. Male, white, mid-40s,
    short red hair, balding in front, brown eyes,
    6'2", 175 lbs., freckles under his eyes, wearing a
    faded olive drab T-shirt, faded blue denim pants,
    and dirty white tennis shoes with no socks.

    BETTY LUNNER, Sgt., Wallowa Police Department.
```

Figure 4-3. Example of <u>MENTIONED</u> format

written under <u>MENTIONED</u> after the person's name and status. A few brief lines of information concerning how to locate this person may save hours of effort later on. When writing additional information in the <u>MENTIONED</u> section about how to locate a particular person, concentrate on writing the names, addresses, and phone numbers of people who know that person well, e.g., good friends, employers, landladies, coworkers, relatives, even ex-spouses and parole officers.

At times a person is not identified by name but is nevertheless likely to be important to the case as a witness or as a suspect. This person may be listed in <u>MENTIONED</u> as unidentified and a description given. It is important that the person who gave the description be mentioned in either <u>ACTION TAKEN</u> or <u>STATEMENTS</u> as the source of that description. See Figure 4-3.

The purpose for listing names under <u>MENTIONED</u> is two-fold: first, to aid others (detectives, process servers, etc.) in locating witnesses more easily; second, to introduce readers to the people whose names will appear in the narrative. Thus the readers will be able to follow the report more easily, much like the cast of characters at the beginning of a play, as in Figure 4-4.

```
MONTAGUE, Romeo's father
ROMEO, Montague's son and Juliet's lover
LADY MONTAGUE, wife to Montague
ABRAM, servant to Montague
BALTHASAR, servant to Romeo
ESCALUS, Prince of Verona
PARIS, a young count, kinsman to the Prince
MERCUTIO, kinsman to the Prince and friend to
Romeo
BENVOLIO, nephew to Montague and friend to Romeo
CAPULET, Juliet's father
JULIET, Capulet's daughter and Romeo's lover
LADY CAPULET, wife to Capulet
TYBALT, nephew to Lady Capulet
SAMPSON, servant to Capulet
GREGORY, servant to Capulet
PETER, servant to Juliet's nurse
FRIAR JOHN, a Franciscan
FRIAR LAWRENCE, a Franciscan
(and others)
```

Figure 4-4. The list of people in MENTIONED is similar to a list of characters in a play.

4.3 ACTION TAKEN

The first thing written under ACTION TAKEN is the word "On," followed by the date, time of the dispatch call, and the arrival time, as in Figure 4-5.

Next follows the officer's activities and observations in the order those things took place. Writing in chronological order is the easiest way to describe the investigation. It is also the easiest way for the reader to understand what the officer did and the reasons for the officer's actions and observations. The officer should describe what was detected by the senses (sight, hearing, smell, taste, touch).

```
ACTION TAKEN
    On October 12, 19—, at 11:37 P.M. I was
dispatched to 3754 S. St. Paul Blvd., concern-
ing a prowler. I arrived at 11:42 P.M.
```

Figure 4-5. Example of a first sentence in ACTION TAKEN

> I went to the back door with Deputy Nicola and
> knocked loudly. Deputy Nicola told me that he
> had seen a man with a yellow shirt in the
> kitchen as we walked toward the back door, so I
> knocked again. I told Deputy Nicola to return
> to the patrol car and call for assistance.
> Deputy Nicola returned in a few minutes and
> told me that the neighbor to the east had told
> him that...

Figure 4-6. Describing another officer's actions in ACTION TAKEN

As the officer describes various activities and observations, other officers' actions may also be discussed, as in Figure 4-6. It must be clear, however, how the officer learned of the others' actions.

When referring to other officers' activities, it is often sufficient to describe their function in general terms (e.g., provided cover, took photographs, interviewed neighbors, directed traffic, lifted latent prints). In the event the other officer detected a fact that no one else did or did as well, that other officer will of course also write a narrative report. Usually the other officer's report will be short, relating only to a single observation or two.

As the officer progresses from one activity to another, it is important that the reasons for the different activities and observations be explained in the narrative report. Often the reasons are apparent without a specific written

> After I finished taking pictures of the damage
> to the 1989 Honda motorcycle, I drove to Mrs.
> Udovich's home in Elgin to examine her Chrysler
> sedan again.
>
> I did this because when I was taking pictures
> of the motorcycle, I saw paint transfers on the
> rear wheel, frame, and tail pipe that matched
> the paint and damage that I'd noticed on Mrs.
> Udovich's Chrysler when it was impounded in an
> unrelated case. The damage on the Chrysler did
> seem to be consistent with it having struck a
> motorcycle.

Figure 4-7. Explaining the reason for an activity in ACTION TAKEN

> I introduced myself to Mr. Rikkula and inter-
> viewed him. Then I returned to the barn with
> Trooper Merkle and began looking for more
> stolen car parts.

Figure 4-8. Briefly mentioning the fact of an interview in <u>ACTION TAKEN</u>

explanation. When an explanation is needed, it is usually something the officer heard or saw and must be written out as the reason for the officer's next activity, as in Figure 4-7. This not only makes the report easier to understand, the officer also appears more organized and methodical.

Statements of people ordinarily should not be written out in any detail in the <u>ACTION TAKEN</u> section. However, that an interview occurred or that a statement was taken must be briefly mentioned here, as in Figure 4-8.

The only exception to this rule (that statements are not to be written in <u>ACTION TAKEN</u>) is when the officer took further action as a direct result of a statement heard. The officer then need mention only as much of the statement as will allow the reader to understand why further action was taken. This brief statement heard by the officer is best written in <u>ACTION TAKEN</u> at the time the interview is mentioned, if that statement was the reason for the officer's very next action, as in Figure 4-9.

> I finished talking to Mr: McLennan about the
> missing coin and returned to my patrol car
> where Ms. Axom was waiting for me. Ms. Axom
> told me that she'd seen Mr. McLennan take a
> small shiny object from his shirt pocket just
> as I'd turned and walked away from him. Ms.
> Axom said that Mr. McLennan put the object in
> his right shoe.
>
> I went back to Mr. McLennan and asked him to
> take off his right shoe.

Figure 4-9. Statements explaining actions in <u>ACTION TAKEN</u>

> While talking to the owner of the hardware
> store, I noticed that there were lockers in the
> employees' lunchroom and that employees' names
> were painted on their lockers. I remembered that
> when I had spoken on Thursday with the kidnap
> victim, Mr. Jurgens, he told me that the shorter
> of the two kidnappers had mentioned having a
> locker in the lunchroom where he worked.

Figure 4-10. Statements explaining observations in <u>ACTION TAKEN</u>

On the other hand, the brief explanatory statement is best written out later in the report when it is the reason for later action by the officer, as in Figure 4-10.

Evidence should not be detailed under the <u>ACTION TAKEN</u> section. However, the fact of evidence being seized or obtained should be mentioned here briefly, as in Figure 4-11.

(A full discussion of how to report the collection of physical evidence is given later in this chapter.)

Greater detail should be given under <u>ACTION TAKEN</u> whenever the investigation into the crime yields any of the following elements.

A Search, Seizure, Stop, Frisk, or Arrest
The United States Constitution and almost all state constitutions contain provisions that restrict a government official's ability to search and seize a citizen's

> Officer Chapman read Mr. Kinser his rights from
> a Miranda card, which Officer Chapman then
> dated and initialed. I took photographs of the
> burns on Mr. Kinser's hands and arms and seized
> his shoes. Then I asked Mr. Kinser if I could
> have his permission to search his 1977
> Chevrolet, and he said, "OK." I searched his
> car and removed a can of gasoline from the
> trunk, along with a 12-gauge shotgun with the
> stock sawed off and taped with a loop so that
> the shotgun could be hung from the shoulder.

Figure 4-11. Briefly mentioning evidence in <u>ACTION TAKEN</u>

person, papers, or property without a warrant and without probable cause, also known as good reason. These restrictions apply to arrests, stop and frisk situations, as well as to searches and seizures. Police officers who violate these provisions do so at a very high cost: not only the loss of valuable evidence seized at the time, but also the possible suppression of statements and the possible suppression of derivative evidence discovered as a direct result of the information obtained during the bad search, arrest, or stop.

In order to act within these constitutional restrictions, officers are merely required to act reasonably. Of course what constitutes acting reasonably is the subject of much debate and is far too broad a topic for this text. However, for narrative report writing purposes, there is a simple solution. The writer must write out in detail the reasons for each stop, frisk, search, seizure, or arrest, as in Figure 4-12.

An Element of the Crime

Every legislature enacts criminal laws for its own state. In doing so, the legislature not only chooses the conduct that will be prohibited but also makes important language and word choices in describing that conduct. It is common

```
From the previous shift's roll call bulletin,
I recognized Mr. Patterson's name and that he
was the suspect in a series of recent armed
robberies in which a handgun was used. Mr.
Patterson was very nervous when I stopped him
although I had explained to him that it was
only for an improper turn.

Mr. Patterson kept touching his right hand
jacket pocket, which appeared to contain a
bulky object about the size of a handgun. When
I asked Mr. Patterson what he had in his
pocket, he said, "Nothing."

I ordered Mr. Patterson to face his car, place
his hands on the roof, and step back. I patted
Mr. Patterson's jacket pocket and felt a hard
object in his right jacket pocket. I reached
into his pocket and took out a .22 caliber
semiautomatic pistol. I told Mr. Patterson
that he was under arrest for carrying a
concealed weapon.
```

Figure 4-12. Giving detailed reasons for "stop, frisk, and search" in <u>ACTION TAKEN</u>

for legislation to define very carefully some of the words and phrases used in the criminal laws. These laws and definitions differ from state to state. For example, what constitutes "property" for theft purposes in one state may be defined differently in another state. One state may define property as including services performed, whereas another state may exclude services from the definition of property.

Despite the many differences in criminal laws among states, there are two constants that apply to all crimes in all states. First, criminal laws are made up of "elements." Second, there are common or recurring themes among these elements. These themes typically involve such things as weapon usage or possession, injury caused or threatened, dollar amount of loss or damage, mental state with which the suspect acted (e.g., intentionally or recklessly), and identification of the suspect as the person responsible.

Whenever the investigation bears on an element of a crime, the goal is to learn as much as possible about what the witnesses saw and heard concerning that element. The goal of the report writer is to write a narrative report that explains what the witnesses saw and heard concerning that element.

In Oregon, for example, if a person steals less than $500 from a convenience store clerk, the crime would be misdemeanor theft if no force was used or threatened against the clerk. If force was used or threatened, however, the crime would be a class C felony, Robbery in the Third Degree. If the force included the use of a baseball bat in such a way that it became a "dangerous weapon" as defined in ORS 161.015(1), the crime would be a very serious class A felony, Robbery in the First Degree. In such a case the officer would determine from the victim and witnesses if force was used or threatened. If so, the officer would determine if the baseball bat was used, attempted to be used, or threatened to be used in a way that it would be readily capable of causing death or serious physical injury (the statutory definition of dangerous weapon).

The witnesses to the convenience store crime would be interviewed extensively to learn exactly what the suspect did and said during the robbery. The officer must then write in the narrative report the statements of those people with firsthand knowledge. It is important that the officer go into great detail as to what the witnesses said concerning force and weapon.

This same detail is important when writing in the narrative concerning any element of the crime.

Defenses to the Crime

Whenever it appears that the suspect may have a defense to the crime, such as intoxication, alibi, insanity, self-defense, etc., the narrative report must be specific and detailed about the facts that support or contradict this defense.

Of course the focus of the inquiry and the information that will be included in the narrative report will differ with the type of defense suggested by the facts of the case. The defense of insanity, for example, is suggested when the suspect's actions and statements before, during, and after the crime are bizarre and seem to make no sense. That defense is available when the suspect, having committed a criminal act, was suffering from a mental disease or defect and therefore was unable to understand that such conduct was wrong or was unable to act lawfully.

Typical areas of inquiry and information to be included in the report in such cases are

1. Were there understandable, logical (although unusual) reasons for what the suspect did?
2. Did the suspect report hearing voices?
3. Did the suspect carry on normal activities requiring thought, planning, logic, and conformance to social norms around the time of the criminal act (writing checks, changing oil, working, visiting sick friends, studying for a test, filling out government forms, etc.)?
4. Did the suspect's relatives and friends think the suspect suffered from a mental problem? Why?
5. Does the suspect have a history of mental problems?
6. Is there an alternative explanation for the suspect's bizarre behavior (anger, alcohol, etc.)?

The defense of intoxication is suggested when the suspect had been ingesting intoxicants just prior to the criminal act. This defense is available when the ingestion of legal or illegal substances caused the suspect to be unable to form the specific intent required for the crime involved. For example, if because of being intoxicated, the suspect was unable to form the intent to steal when entry was made into another person's house, the crime of burglary was not committed. Burglary requires breaking in with the intent to commit a crime in the house (e.g., theft).

When I arrested Mr. Loftis in the bathroom of
the residence at 1:40 A.M., I noticed that he
had a heavy odor of alcoholic beverage about
his breath, that his walk was unsteady, and
that his speech was slightly slurred. As I led
him out of the bathroom, he staggered against
the sink and the door frame and walked halt-
ingly to my patrol car.

He was wearing black clothing and dark gloves.
In his back pocket he had a 13"-long screwdriver with a standard tip. It appeared to
match the marks on the aluminum frame of the
sliding glass patio door which I'd examined
earlier because it appeared to be the point of
entry during the burglary. The marks were on
the outside of the door next to the lock, and
Mr. Wurtting, the homeowner, told me that the
marks were not there before the burglary.

I also found three rings in Mr. Loftis's right
front pants pocket. Mr. Wurtting identified
them as belonging to his wife and said the
rings had been on their dresser when they
retired for the evening at about 11:00 P.M.

Figure 4-13. Details reported in <u>ACTION TAKEN</u> regarding intoxication defense

However, merely because the suspect was under the influence when entry was made into the house does not mean there was no intent to steal. There must be more information gathered by the investigating officer concerning the suspect's conduct and demeanor at the time of the criminal act.

In the case of a suspect who had been drinking and was arrested for burglary at the scene, the officer may well write a report, in part, as illustrated in Figure 4-13.

Injuries to a Person in Custody

If any injuries occur to a person in custody, the circumstances should be included in the report, as in Figure 4-14. This is because of the high likelihood that a claim for damages may be made against the officer or the department by the injured person.

I placed Mrs. Hoff in the rear of my patrol car.
She was handcuffed with her hands behind her and
appeared to be in no pain and made no complaint
of pain to me, nor did she have any marks,
bruises, or blood on her. As I got in the
driver's seat, preparing to drive to the jail, I
heard a loud thump and looked around and saw
that Mrs. Hoff was on her knees on the seat
facing the right rear door window and was bang-
ing her forehead against the glass. I had not
yet started the car and had heard nothing from
Mrs. Hoff to warn me that she might try to hurt
herself. I immediately ran to her door and
opened it. She had hit her forehead against the
glass at least four times before I could get her
door open and stop her. The window glass was not
broken but had blood on the inside surface and
Mrs. Hoff's forehead was cut and bleeding.

Figure 4-14. Details reported in <u>ACTION TAKEN</u> regarding injuries to an arrested person

4.4 <u>STATEMENTS</u>

Witnesses

Only those witnesses who have been interviewed should be included under
<u>STATEMENTS</u>. The name of the witness should be capitalized and underlined,
and the words "told me" follow the name. A one- or two-sentence introduction
explaining the witness's relationship to the case should be written after "told
me," as in Figure 4-15.

<u>STATEMENTS</u>
    <u>JAMES DAVID PEAKE</u> told me that he was a sopho-
more at the University of Colorado and was
hitchhiking back to school when his last ride
left him off at Pilot Rock so that he could
catch another ride. It was about 3:00 P.M., and
he was standing in front of Morrow's grocery
store when he heard...

Figure 4-15. Example of reporting a witness's statement in <u>STATEMENTS</u>

The officer should then write out what the witness said. This should be written in chronological order as the events happened from the witness's point of view, not in the order the witness related them to the officer. The concern is that the witness's firsthand view of the events be explained in the most understandable form (chronological order) once the officer understands what the witness saw and heard.

Of course if during the interview with the witness, the officer determines that the witness has intentionally made a false statement, the officer should report both the false statement as well as the true fact as learned by the officer. The officer must be sure to report those intentional falsehoods in this way, but only when the officer is sure there was not a mistake due to an innocent failure to communicate accurately.

The witness's statement should be written out in the <u>STATEMENTS</u> section of the report in some detail. When a written or taped statement has been obtained, the <u>STATEMENTS</u> section of the report need only contain a summarized version of the witness's statement. Of course in the case of a written or taped statement, the <u>ACTION TAKEN</u> section will contain a reference to the fact that the written or taped statement was obtained. That written or taped statement will be listed in the <u>EVIDENCE</u> section.

The officer should be aware when interviewing witnesses that something the witness is saying may not have been known by the witness personally but was something told to that witness by someone else. If this is the case, include in that witness's statement the name of the person from whom the witness got the information firsthand, as in Figure 4-16.

```
    Mr. Herblacht told me that his plant foreman,
    Mr. Perkins, had told him that when he got to
    work he noticed that the company truck had been
    broken into. Mr. Perkins told him that the
    usual driver of that truck, Mr. Myers, looked
    the truck over and saw that a radio and a tool-
    box had been taken.
```

Figure 4-16. Showing the source of a witness's information in <u>STATEMENTS</u>

Anytime a witness reports the actual words spoken by a suspect to the witness or overheard by the witness, the report must, if possible, quote the actual words exactly as said by the suspect (according to the witness). Quotation marks must be used in those cases, but otherwise, quotations should rarely be written in the <u>STATEMENTS</u> section of narrative reports. (See chapter 5 for further information on the proper use of quotations.)

An example of a properly written <u>STATEMENTS</u> section may be found in the narrative example in the appendix.

Suspects

Any statements made by the suspect should be included under the major heading <u>STATEMENTS</u>. However, the style for writing the suspect's statement is substantially different than that used for the witness's statement.

The suspect's name should be capitalized and underlined, and the word "suspect" then follows. The remainder of the lead paragraph should include

1. The date, time, and place of the interview.
2. Who was present during the interview.
3. When and how the Miranda rights were given and the response. If the Miranda rights were not given, the lead paragraph should explain the reasons why they were not given. The most common reason for not giving the Miranda rights to the suspect before the interview is because the suspect was not in custody at the time. The suspect may not have been in custody for a variety of reasons. For example, the officer did not make an arrest and did not intend to make an arrest, regardless of what the suspect may have said during the interview.

Examples of how the lead paragraph of a suspect's statement may be written are shown in Figure 4-17.

After the first paragraph the succeeding paragraphs then give the substance of the suspect's statement. The substance of the interview with the suspect is written differently than is the interview with witnesses. The suspect's interview is written chronologically as things were told to the officer by the suspect. (The interview with the witness is written chronologically as events happened from the witness's point of view.)

```
STATEMENTS
     WILLIAM E. MOLLER, suspect. I interviewed Mr.
Moller at 8:30 P.M. on June 12, 19——, in my
office at the Amity Police Department. We were
alone. I first read him his Miranda rights from
a card and when I asked him if he understood
his rights, he said, "Yeah, I do."
```

OR

```
STATEMENTS
     WILLIAM E. MOLLER, suspect. I interviewed Mr.
Moller at 8:30 P.M. on June 12, 19——, in my
office at the Amity Police Department. We were
alone. I had telephoned him just before noon to
ask him if he'd meet with me to discuss a matter
concerning a young girl in his neighborhood who
had reported a crime. He said he was working
until 7:00 P.M. and didn't get home until 7:30
P.M. He asked if we could meet at 8:30 P.M. I
agreed. He appeared at about 8:25 P.M., and I
met him at the counter in the lobby. I asked him
if he minded talking in my office and he said,
"Not at all." I got two soft drinks and gave one
to Mr. Moller as he'd said he was thirsty. Once
in my office, I told Mr. Moller he was free to
leave and regardless of what he told me, I would
not take him to jail that day because I had not
yet completed the investigation. I just wanted
his side of the story.
```

Figure 4-17. Two sample lead paragraphs reporting the suspect's statements in STATEMENTS

See Figure 4-18 for an example of how to report the substance of an interview with a suspect.

Anytime a suspect makes an important statement that has a bearing on the crime, it is best to quote exactly what was said. Should the suspect confess to committing the crime, always report in detail what led up to the confession. Often a suspect will not tell the truth at first but will decide to confess after the officer has pointed out an inconsistent statement or a particularly strong piece of evidence showing that the suspect committed the crime (e.g., suspect's fingerprints found in the victim's house). This detail about what caused the

> Mr. Moller told me that he'd never touched
> Veronica. I asked him who he was talking about,
> and he said, "Aren't you asking me about Veronica
> Smathers?" I asked him what made him think that
> Veronica Smathers had accused him of anything,
> and he became flustered and stammered, "I thought
> you...didn't she...uh, this is too much...."

Figure 4-18. Sample paragraph of a suspect's interview in <u>STATEMENTS</u>

suspect to decide to confess is very persuasive information and must be written in detail in the narrative report, as in Figure 4-19.

In the event a suspect does not confess or admit anything at all but lies to the officer, the officer's report must be specific in reporting what the suspect said that was not true. Often a lie told by a suspect during an interview is as effective a piece of evidence as is a confession (if the statement can be proven to be a lie).

> Mr. Osbourne told me that he didn't start any
> fire, that he was just in the area and happened
> to see the fire so he stopped to see if the fire
> department would arrive. I asked him how long
> he'd waited and watched before the fire depart-
> ment arrived and he said, "About a minute." I
> looked at him for fifteen seconds, saying noth-
> ing, and he said, "Well, maybe ten minutes." I
> told him that that was a big difference in time
> and he needed to be sure. I also told him that he
> didn't get the singed jacket by just watching and
> also that he smelled of gasoline. He looked away
> from me and I saw his chin quiver. After about
> twenty seconds he said, "I'm really sorry I did
> it. I need help. I don't know why I did it."

Figure 4-19. Reporting a suspect's confession in <u>STATEMENTS</u>

4.5 EVIDENCE

Physical items that are collected during the investigation of a criminal case tend to be of great value at the trial of that case. An oral description of a bloody knife, for example, does not have the emotional impact of the bloody knife itself. The presence of physical exhibits at the trial tends to eliminate disputes or arguments. A controversy about whether an eyewitness had the ability to see across a yard containing trees and shrubs is resolved when a photograph taken from the eyewitness's vantage point is produced in court.

The EVIDENCE section lists all physical items collected or created during the investigative period covered by the narrative report. The items to be listed include not only things collected, e.g., guns, clothing, vehicles, stolen property, drugs, etc., but also things created by the officer's activities, e.g., Miranda rights cards, written statements, photographs, latent print cards, photo displays, diagrams, cassette tapes of recorded statements, etc.

All of these things are listed under the EVIDENCE section, which is written in a four-column format, using the following headings:

```
EVIDENCE
    ITEM        LOCATION      SEIZED BY    DISPOSITION
    latent      crime         myself       Property
    prints      scene                      No. 161 B-23

    bill of     glovebox      Mr. Yanos    No. 10 E-2
    sale        of 1972       and myself
                Ford LXH871

    Miranda     in front of   myself       No. 14 L-6
    rights      Mr. Torres's
    card        residence

    pocket      Mr. Torres's  Trooper      No. 14 R-2
    watch       right front   Tolen
                pocket
```

Figure 4-20. Example of the proper EVIDENCE format

1. <u>ITEM</u>: Describe the item seized.
2. <u>LOCATION</u>: Describe the location from which the item was recovered after the crime occurred.
3. <u>SEIZED BY</u>: Name the person who first recovered the item and the person to whom it was given, if applicable.
4. <u>DISPOSITION</u>: Tell what was done with the item by way of storage or safekeeping.

See Figure 4-20 for an example of a proper <u>EVIDENCE</u> format.

No item of physical evidence, with some minor exceptions, can be admitted into evidence at trial unless a witness identifies it. Making sure that a witness will be able to identify the item later in court is an important part of evidence collection. This is easily done in most cases by having the witness sign or initial and date the item soon after it is seized.

The witnesses who seize the items should be listed in the <u>SEIZED BY</u> column.

4.6 <u>ACTION RECOMMENDED</u>

Finish up the report with whatever investigative action, if any, still needs to be taken. If nothing is left to be done, write "None" under the <u>ACTION RECOM-MENDED</u> heading.

An example where further investigative activity is recommended is shown in Figure 4-21.

```
ACTION RECOMMENDED
      Interview Mr. Dawes again concerning Mr.
      Swope's alibi for the evening of July 13, 19—.
      Send the latent prints to the identification
      bureau to be compared with Mr. Swope's prints.
```

Figure 4-21. Example of a typical <u>ACTION RECOMMENDED</u> format

4.7 SO YOU LEFT
SOMETHING OUT?

A common experience among narrative report writers who handwrite or type their reports is that they sometimes finish writing a section of the narrative and then discover they have left something out. Instead of rewriting the narrative report, it is a very simple matter to place an asterisk (*) at the point in the narrative where the portion was left out. Then the officer will complete the narrative. After ACTION RECOMMENDED the officer will place a second asterisk and then write in the missing information. See the narrative report example in the appendix for an example of the use of an asterisk to include something at the very end of the narrative report that was inadvertently omitted from the body of the narrative.

Report writers who use a word processor to write their reports can easily insert omitted material at the appropriate place before the report is printed.

SUMMARY

The detailed rules for writing the content of each of the six sections (SUMMARY, MENTIONED, ACTION TAKEN, STATEMENTS, EVIDENCE, and ACTION RECOMMENDED) are quite specific. This preserves the integrity of each section, as each has its own specific function that exactly addresses critical elements necessary for a good narrative report.

Those critical elements spring from the theme that a good narrative report concentrates on writing about witnesses and not just on collecting facts. The following guide condenses the rules and sets out critical elements for writing the narrative report.

SUMMARY (the introduction)	"On," plus the date, time, place of the event being investigated.
MENTIONED (cast of characters)	Names and status and, if necessary, further information about how to locate a particular witness.

ACTION TAKEN (writer's statement)	"On," plus the date and times of dispatch and arrival; followed by officer's chronological account of investigative activities and observations and the reasons therefore; no detail given as to statements taken or evidence seized.
STATEMENTS (people interviewed)	<u>Witnesses</u>: Name and "told me," followed by chronological events as they happened to the witness. <u>Suspects</u>: Name and "suspect." Lead paragraph gives date, time, place of interview, and who was present, plus Miranda warnings and responses (or why Miranda warnings were not given). Subsequent paragraphs contain a title (e.g., Miss, Ms., Mrs. or Mr.), followed by the last name. Then "told me" is followed by the statement of the suspect in chronological order as told by the suspect.
EVIDENCE (physical things)	Four columns: <u>ITEM</u>, <u>LOCATION</u>, <u>SEIZED BY</u>, <u>DISPOSITION</u>; filled in so the writer explains each physical object — where it came from, and most importantly who first seized it.
ACTION RECOMMENDED (what's next)	The next investigative step is suggested.

▼ REVIEW QUESTIONS

1. Explain the purposes for each of the six narrative report sections: <u>SUMMARY</u>, <u>MENTIONED</u>, <u>ACTION TAKEN</u>, <u>STATEMENTS</u>, <u>EVIDENCE</u>, <u>ACTION RECOMMENDED</u>.
2. In which narrative report sections does the word "On" appear as the lead word?
3. In which sections are the date and time of dispatch written?
4. What are the three different ways a crime report <u>SUMMARY</u> refers to the person who committed the crime?
5. Explain how to determine the "significant event" for the <u>SUMMARY</u> of a follow-up report.

6. Which parts of the narrative report are written in chronological order?
7. What is the reason for the rule that statements are not written in any detail in <u>ACTION TAKEN</u>? Explain the exception to that rule.
8. When is it necessary for the officer to write some portions of the narrative report in more detail than others?
9. Why are statements of witnesses reported differently than are statements of suspects?
10. Explain the reasons for each of the four columns in the <u>EVIDENCE</u> section.
11. If you finish writing the entire narrative report and find that you left out something important, explain how to include the missing part without rewriting the narrative.

▼ WRITING DRILLS

1. Using only the important facts from the following information, write a proper <u>SUMMARY</u> section.

   During your investigation of a knifepoint robbery, Gerald Roger Sullivan told you that as he was closing up his gas station at 2212 Western Street, Vale, a young man wearing a ski mask and brandishing a knife entered the office and took the shift's receipts from him. The robber then ran off telling Mr. Sullivan that if he followed him, he'd be killed. The robbery happened at 11:50 P.M. on March 12, 19—. The investigation did not reveal any information about the identity of the robber.

2. Using only the important facts from the following information, write a proper <u>SUMMARY</u> section.

   Michelle Kae Tegg, age 10, was interviewed by you on May 3, 19— concerning a sexual abuse incident. She told you that Roland Bates, a man who lived two doors from her at 1004 Veronica Street, Winston, invited her into his house at about 9:30 A.M. that day. She went in and about 10 minutes later he suddenly pushed her down on the couch and fondled her breasts. She began to cry and he stopped and said he was sorry. She ran home and told her mother who called the police. You attempted to locate Mr. Bates but found that he was not home.

3. Using only the important facts from the following information, write a proper <u>SUMMARY</u> section.

You arrested Bonnie Mae Mathers of 1771 SW Taylor Court, Powers, at 3:30 P.M. on July 19, 19—. You made the arrest at the conclusion of your investigation of a shoplifting crime. Mrs. Mathers had been stopped by the store security personnel on that same day at 2:55 P.M. She tried to leave Brower's Drug Store, 2781 SE Banner Street, Prineville, with a portable television set she hadn't paid for. You lodged her in the local county jail.

4. Using only the important facts from the following information, write a proper <u>SUMMARY</u> section.

On February 2, 19—, in the early morning hours (between 1:00 A.M. and 3:00 A.M.) an unoccupied house at 7121 N. Glazier Street, Applegate, was burned. During the subsequent arson investigation, you interviewed an eyewitness, Thomas Albert Unger, at the Applegate Police Department at about 9:30 A.M. on February 17, 19—. Mr. Unger told you that he had seen a man start the fire and gave a complete physical description of that man and of the man's car.

5. Using only the important facts from the following information, write a proper <u>MENTIONED</u> section.

During the investigation period covered by your report, you interviewed three people — Kaofo Saecho (the suspect), Remo Gene Churchill (a victim), and Sandra Carlene Merill (another victim). All three persons' addresses, dates of birth, and phone numbers are set forth on the facesheet. However, Mr. Churchill told you that his current address is only temporary as he had just separated from his wife and was staying with a friend while he looked for a permanent place. His friend will know where he will be. His friend's name was Todd Fechter. Also while interviewing Mr. Saecho, he told you that he believed that the night watchman, Monte, saw him commit the crime. From Mr. Saecho's description of Monte, you know that his full name is Monte Radke and that he works for Allied Security, 8187 SW Pine Street, Wilderville, 371-3732.

6. Write a paragraph or two for the <u>ACTION TAKEN</u> section, incorporating the following described activities into the paragraphs and adding information (you will have to make it up) that explains the reasons for your activities.

You saw a 1979 Plymouth parked beside Highway 26 just south of the Farmsville Road intersection. You stopped because (provide a reason). While looking into the car from the outside, you saw a purse and a baby blanket with what appeared to be blood all over it. You opened the car door and looked inside the purse to see if you could locate anything that would identify the people who had been in the vehicle because (provide a reason). While looking in the purse, you found a baggie of what appeared to be cocaine.

7. Rewrite the following information in the correct chronological order for the <u>ACTION TAKEN</u> section of the report.

During your investigation of an incident where Doris Bauer sold heroin to an undercover police officer, you arrested Mrs. Bauer just after the buy took place. You also seized the buy money from her after she was handcuffed and placed in the patrol car. The entire buy had been videotaped by you. The videotape was also seized by you. Prior to the buy, the undercover officer, Trooper Frasca, drove to Zale's Brothers parking lot. He got into the passenger's side of Mrs. Bauer's car. You saw him give the signal that the buy had taken place, and other officers approached the car and had Mrs. Bauer get out of the car at gunpoint. The surveillance of Mrs. Bauer's car in the parking lot began at 9:30 P.M. on September 12, 19—, and Trooper Frasca made the buy at 9:40 P.M.

8. Write a paragraph or two for the <u>ACTION TAKEN</u> section, incorporating the following described activities and adding information (you will have to make it up) that explains the reasons for your activities.
    a) You interviewed the victim of a burglary, Jennifer Martin.
    b) Next you went to Ms. Martin's neighbor, Arnold B. Theeler, because (provide a reason).
    c) Then you returned to Ms. Martin's home and searched the bushes next to the garage because (provide a reason).
    d) From among the things you saw in the bushes, you seized an empty red and white aluminum soft drink can because (provide a reason).

9. Using only the important facts from the following information, write a proper <u>STATEMENTS</u> section concerning a witness interview.

During a particularly difficult interview with a distraught mother of a kidnapped child you learned that the mother, Frances Loy Cross, had just lost her husband to an industrial accident a month earlier. On

April 12, 19—, she had her first real outing since his death. She took her 11-month-old daughter, Cindy, to the Aumsville Mall in a stroller, arriving at 2:30 P.M. Mrs. Cross first stopped by the phone company to pay her phone bill and then she walked to the crafts store. Mrs. Cross had a difficult time answering your questions as she was crying and continually asking where her baby was. Finally she calmed herself and was able to tell you what happened. However, when she mentioned the crafts store and what happened there, Mrs. Cross broke down again and was unable to continue for several minutes. Finally she was able to tell you that the reason for her losing control when discussing the crafts store was because her last fond memories of her husband concerned a craft class they had been taking at the store the day before his death. After composing herself again, she told you that she'd had a premonition that something awful was going to happen to her daughter that day. Mrs. Cross said she'd even talked it over with her pastor the day before. She said that she was in the crafts store with her daughter in the stroller and that she walked away from the stroller for two minutes. She returned and found both her daughter and the stroller gone. They had been next to the satin bow display. Mrs. Cross immediately searched the whole store and when she couldn't find her daughter or the stroller, the manager of the store called the police. In answer to your question, Mrs. Cross said, "It was just after 3:00 P.M. when I found Cindy missing."

10. Using only the important facts from the following information, write a proper <u>STATEMENTS</u> section concerning an interview with a suspect. During the execution of a search warrant for stolen car parts, you were assigned the responsibility for interviewing people who came to the door of the mobile home being searched. One person who came to the door was Jamie Cassner, a 20-year-old male whom you knew to be a suspected car thief. You were in the mobile home when you saw Mr. Cassner drive up in a blue 1989 Corvette convertible and approach the door of the mobile home. You walked out and met him on the porch and identified yourself as a police officer. Mr. Cassner asked what was going on and you told him that the mobile home was being searched under the authority of a search warrant. You asked him what business he had there and he became nervous and said he was lost and just stopped to ask directions. You told him that you may be able to help and asked where he wanted to go. He stammered and said he was looking for a girl's house. He couldn't give an address, phone number, or even the name of the girl. He said

she was blonde and that's all he knew about her, except that she lived on the same street where the mobile home was located. You pointed out to Mr. Cassner that the street was a dead-end street and there were only two other houses. When you pointed out that the girl obviously lived in one of those two other houses, Mr. Cassner, speaking very rapidly, said he didn't think that was true and he must have the wrong street and he'd just forget about her. When you said you'd walk him to his car because it was such a nice one and you'd like to look at it, Mr. Cassner got more nervous and said he didn't like people looking at it. You told him that sometimes people steal nice cars like that one by hot-wiring them, and Mr. Cassner blurted out that in fact it was hot-wired because he lost the key. You asked him if it was stolen and he said, "I think it's hot all right; a guy I met give it to me to drive for a while." At that point you advised Mr. Cassner of his Miranda rights and continued to question him.

11. Using only the important facts from the following information, write a proper EVIDENCE section.

    During a consent search of a 1983 Datsun, you found a sealed box containing twenty-four expensive ink pens on the right rear floor-board covered with a blanket. While you were lifting latent prints from the steering wheel and rear view mirror, Officer Gregor told you that he had just interviewed Barbara Tollen and that she had given him an ornate cigarette lighter which she said she'd gotten from Charles Rawley (the suspect). You seized the lighter as evidence as you realized that it was the same lighter that belonged to Bernie Siegel (the victim). Officer Gregor also took several photographs of the 1983 Datsun at your request.

CHAPTER FIVE

▼

How to Write Clearly, Objectively, and Effectively

5.1 WRITING CLEARLY

"I"

The most effective writing is direct and to the point. It avoids formal, stilted, or awkward language. It is writing that uses the type of language most of us use in our everyday spoken language.

In the past, police officers commonly used the words "writer," "undersigned," "this officer," "this reporting officer," "R/O," etc., when referring to themselves

---

The Miranda rights were read.

The marijuana was seized.

The house was entered.

The defendant was heard to say . . .

Figure 5-1. Examples of passive voice

```
I read the Miranda rights.

Officer Barnes seized the marijuana.

Deputy O'Neil entered the house.

I heard the defendant say . . .
```

Figure 5-2. Examples of active voice

in their narrative reports. This artificial type of language should be avoided in favor of the clear and direct "I."

Active versus Passive Voice

There are two sections* in the narrative report where the use of the passive voice must be avoided: <u>ACTION TAKEN</u> and <u>STATEMENTS</u>. It is primarily in these two sections where the reader learns which witness will testify to what facts. Therefore it is important to not only report the fact but also identify the witness who can testify to that fact. The use of the passive voice in these two sections describes the fact but neglects to identify the witness. For example, "The gun was seized" (passive voice) clearly describes the fact but makes it impossible to tell who will testify that the gun was seized. On the other hand, "I seized the gun" (active voice) not only clearly describes the fact but also explains who can testify to that fact.

The key to recognizing the passive voice is the words "were" or "was" followed by a verb, as in Figure 5-1. When the passive voice is used, a note of uncertainty is injected into the report. The fact is reported but not the identity of the person who has firsthand knowledge of that fact. Without the identity of that person, there is no way to be certain that the fact can be established in court.

However, when the active voice is used, both the action and the person performing the action are named, as in Figure 5-2. This makes it clear who the witness is who can testify that the activity took place.

*NOTE: None of the other sections of the narrative report require that the active voice be used. In <u>MENTIONED</u> and in <u>EVIDENCE</u> the writing is done by listing things, not by using sentences and paragraphs. <u>SUMMARY</u> and <u>ACTION RECOMMENDED</u> are not intended to be witnesses' statements, only a general factual introduction and a commentary on further investigation needed, respectively.

reported	claimed
indicated	related
inferred	implied
stated	announced
declared	communicated
alleged	maintained
noted	insisted

Figure 5-3. Use "said" or "told me" instead of these words.

"Said" or "Told Me"

In any investigative activity, a police officer will usually talk to many people, several of whom may say things that will need to be written down in the narrative police report. In the past, police officers have drawn from a very wide choice of words to describe that type of communication. Many of the words they have used are listed in Figure 5-3. Though all of these words are useful for other types of writing, they are not as helpful for narrative police reports as are the words "said" and "told me." "Said" and "told me" are short, clear, commonly used, and readily understood. These words do not have slightly different meanings as do such words as "claimed" or "insisted." Furthermore, the use of "said" or "told me" makes it clear that it was an oral communication. That is not as clear with the words "indicated" or "implied," which hint that the communication could have been made by pointing, by a suggestive look, or by veiled meaning from what was left unsaid.

It is far better for the officer to write what happened as simply and as clearly as possible. Let the readers draw their own conclusions from what the officer did and heard. Therefore the only words that should be used are "said" and "told me."

Simple Words

Police report writers tend to use jargon in their spoken and written language, as do most professionals. That language used by police report writers is meaningful to those in the field of law enforcement. However, it is awkward and confusing at times to others.

Do Not Write	Do Write
subsequent	after
commenced	began
displayed	showed
enumerated	listed
terminated	ended
utilized	used
contacted	met
altercation	fight
noted	saw
exited	got out, left
activated	turned on
proceeded	went
observed	saw

Figure 5-4. Use simple words.

The rule for effective report writing is to eliminate the jargon and write in a more simplified language, as in Figure 5-4.

Eliminating the jargon will prevent the type of report found in Figure 5-5.

```
Writer exited his patrol unit and visually
detected suspect Kepler proceed to verbally and
physically indicate his displeasure that writer
had responded to the scene at this particular
time. This was accomplished by suspect Kepler
extending the middle finger of his right hand in
a perpendicular position, while the remainder of
his digits remained in a curled fist-like posi-
tion. At the same time, suspect Kepler utilized
a variety of oral communication signals directed
at this writer, from which this writer ascer-
tained that suspect Kepler's state of mind was
such that he was prepared to engage writer in an
imminent physical confrontation.
```

Figure 5-5. Example of using police jargon

```
As I got out of my patrol car, Mr. Kepler gave
me the finger and cursed me out as if challeng-
ing me to fight.
```

Figure 5-6. The same report from Figure 5-5 with jargon eliminated

The same paragraph, without the jargon, is found in Figure 5-6.

Whenever possible, words in police reports should be specific rather than general, as in Figure 5-7. This allows a clearer picture to be conveyed to the reader. For example, it would be better to write "I saw him get an aluminum baseball bat from the trunk of her car" rather than "I saw him get a weapon from her car."

Other ways to write simply include avoiding weak modifiers such as most, really, very, surely, highly, etc. These weak words only add bulk to the report without adding any concrete information.

Similarly there are many words and phrases that are unnecessary, e.g., generally speaking, for the most part, apparently, and greatly. These words add nothing to the report and should be omitted.

Use Past Tense

At the time a police officer is writing the report, the writing will always be about things that happened in the past. Therefore the past tense will always be used to describe events.

Do Not Write	Do Write
residence	duplex
vehicle	pickup truck
store	grocery store
window	wood sash window
fence	barbed wire fence

Figure 5-7. Use words that are specific.

```
I get the call from the dispatcher at 3:37 P.M.
and arrive at Mr. Meacham's house at 3:42 P.M.,
at which time Mrs. Meacham tells me that Mr.
Meacham has just left.
```

Figure 5-8. It is incorrect to use the present tense when writing a police narrative report.

```
I got the call from the dispatcher at 3:37 P.M.
and arrived at Mr. Meacham's house at 3:42 P.M.,
at which time Mrs. Meacham told me that Mr.
Meacham had just left.
```

Figure 5-9. Use the past tense in writing a police narrative report.

For example, it would be incorrect for an officer to write using the present tense, as in Figure 5-8.

It would be correct to use the past tense, as shown in Figure 5-9.

The use of the present tense is not only unclear, it is also factually wrong. The officer is not currently performing the activity being described; rather it has been done in the past, it is over.

The only time that the present tense should be used in a narrative report is when quoting someone who used the present tense, as in Figure 5-10.

```
I heard him say, "I am going downtown."
```

Figure 5-10. The correct use of the present tense in a police narrative report

Time of Day (A.M./P.M.)

In the narrative report, there are often references to the time of day. The officer has the choice of using military time, 1625 hours, or the more common 4:25 P.M. For most people, military time is unnatural and requires a pause and a mental calculation before the time of day is understood.

Unless there is a policy decision by the officer's department that time of day must be written in military time in the narrative report, the officer should use A.M. and P.M. This is the clearer way of writing and is the way of referring to the time of day that a majority of people use.

As a general rule, it is far better to use words that are readily understood. This also applies when an officer testifies in court. All witnesses should avoid using military time when referring to time of day. Many jurors may not understand what time of day that refers to.

Don't Abbreviate

Words should not be abbreviated in the narrative report for the same reason that police jargon should not be used. Not everyone may understand the abbreviation unless it is commonly used by the general public. Abbreviations should also be avoided because they may be subject to more than one meaning, as in Figure 5-11.

Do Not Write	Do Write
R/O	registered owner reserve officer reporting officer
POE	point of entry point of exit
RR	right rear railroad
NF	nothing further not found
FI	field interview

Figure 5-11. Avoid abbreviations when writing a police narrative report.

5.2 WRITING OBJECTIVELY: PERSONS' NAMES

Names of people who are mentioned in the narrative report should be written out. People should not be referred to as the suspect, witness, victim, subject, and so on, and certainly not by number, as in suspect 1 or victim 2. Instead, their full names should be written out, and thereafter they should be referred to by title (e.g., Dr., Mr., Mrs., Miss, or Ms.) plus last name. It is important to write about all adults in the body of the narrative report by using some title with their names. For example, write "Mr. Thompson" instead of just "Thompson." By treating each person with equal respect by using titles, an officer appears much more objective than when referring to the suspect as "suspect" or as "Jones" but to the witness as "Ms. Adams." An officer should refer to all people on a polite, professional, objective level and call them by last names with the appropriate title.

At times there will be two people with the same last name mentioned in an investigation. For the sake of clarity an officer must differentiate between them in the simplest way possible. The preferable and clearest way to distinguish one from the other is to use the first and last names prefaced by a title (e.g., Mr., Mrs., Miss, or Ms.), as in Figure 5-12.

```
I received a phone call from Mr. Herbert Pick.
He asked me to meet his brother, Thomas Pick, in
Terrebonne on 4th Street at Division at 4:00 P.M.
At 3:45 P.M. I arrived at that location and Mr.
Condon drove up and asked me if I was waiting
for a man named Thomas, and I said I was. Mr.
Condon told me that he would be late. I waited
until 4:45 P.M. when Mr. Herbert Pick drove up
and said his brother wouldn't be coming.
```

Figure 5-12. Proper way to refer to adults by name in a police narrative report

```
I spoke with Mr. Teeples and his seven-year-old
son, Tommy Teeples. Tommy told me that....
```

Figure 5-13. Proper way to refer to juveniles by name in a police narrative report

When referring to juveniles, it is not appropriate to use titles such as "Mr." or "Miss." Rather it is best to refer to them initially by first and last name, and thereafter by first name alone, as in Figure 5-13.

Names of individuals, if written alone or in a list may be written last name first (e.g., Fiebach, John Edward). When the name is written in a sentence, however, the last name should be written last, as in Figure 5-14. In the narrative portion of the police report, the officer should write the way most people talk. No one in conversation puts the last name first when mentioning a person by name.

At times, an officer will be required to refer to people who are not identified by name. An example of this might be found in the case of an attempted theft of a

<u>Do Not Write</u>	<u>Do Write</u>
I interviewed Fiebach, John Edward and Mr. Fiebach told me . . .	I interviewed John Edward Fiebach and Mr. Fiebach told me . . .

Figure 5-14. Do not put the last name first when referring to people in a police narrative report.

car by a thief who is surprised by the victim while in the act of breaking into the car, causing the thief to run away. It is best to refer to such unidentified people by describing a reasonably permanent characteristic they possess. For example, "The man with the ponytail ran off."

When there are two or more unknown suspects, it is not a good idea to refer to them by number (e.g., suspect 1, suspect 2). It is clearer to readers if the suspects are each described in writing as they are typically described in normal conversation. Refer to a reasonably permanent feature each possesses (e.g., older/younger, woman with glasses/woman without glasses, bald man/red-haired man, etc.). See Figure 5-15 for two examples of how to refer to unidentified people.

> Mr. Morrison told me that as the older man ran past him, the younger man opened the car door and looked at Mr. Morrison briefly before he, too, fled.

OR

> I walked toward the back door of the store and as I got within twenty-five feet, I saw a woman with glasses open the door and look at me. Then she went back inside and slammed the door. I walked closer and a taller, thinner woman without glasses ran out and ran east toward 49th Avenue.

Figure 5-15. Proper ways of referring to unidentified persons in a police narrative report

```
I watched Mr. Yamamura close and lock the door
of Gene's Coin Shop. He walked to the parking
lot at 37th and Brittin Road and got into a
brown 1975 Chevrolet. Sergeant Fulkerson ran up
to Mr. Yamamura and asked him to get out of the
car. I asked Mr. Yamamura for identification
and he gave me an Arizona driver's license
identifying him as Masano Yamamura.
```

OR

```
I watched a man, later identified as Masano
Yamamura, close and lock the door of Gene's
Coin Shop. He walked to the parking lot at 37th
and Brittin Road and got into a brown 1975
Chevrolet. Sergeant Fulkerson ran up to Mr.
Yamamura and asked him to get out of the car. I
asked Mr. Yamamura for identification and he
gave me an Arizona driver's license identifying
him as Masano Yamamura.
```

Figure 5-16. Proper way of referring to a later identified person

Very often an officer will see an individual do certain things but will not identify that person until later in the investigation. In describing that individual's
activities in the narrative report, it is proper and preferable to refer to that
person by name even though the officer did not know the person's name until
later. This is because it is a simple matter to explain that the individual was
not identified until later. There are two ways this can be done, as shown in
Figure 5-16.

5.3 WRITING EFFECTIVELY

Quotes

From time to time the officer may be inclined to quote statements made by
others. It is rarely productive to quote anyone unless the words being quoted
were originally spoken by the suspect. When the suspect's words are being

```
DALE JAMES CORINER told me that he was the
assistant manager for PEMCO Finance Company's
branch office in Hebo and usually arrived at
work at 7:45 A.M., but on October 12, 19——, he
was fifteen minutes early. As he parked his car
by the mailbox next to the Fifth Street
entrance, he heard a moaning sound coming from
the hallway of the Chalet Apartments.
```

Figure 5-17. An example of paraphrasing a witness's statement

repeated for the officer by a witness who overheard the suspect, or when the officer personally heard the suspect say the words, they should be quoted. In very few other cases is it advisable for the officer to quote witnesses' words. Instead, paraphrasing is preferable.

The examples given in Figures 5-17 and 5-18 demonstrate how to paraphrase a witness and how to quote a suspect's words, respectively.

There is a reason why a witness's precise language should not be quoted in narrative reports. It is more important to report what the witness meant by what was said than to report the exact words. In other words, it is more important for an officer to understand what happened to the witness or what the witness saw and heard so that the officer can accurately write down the witness's story. It is not as helpful if an officer simply quotes the witness and leaves the understanding of what the witness meant to the reader.

```
I told Mr. Rhodes that I wasn't going to arrest
him, that I only wanted to know his side of the
story. He said, "I don't remember even being in
that area of town." I asked if he could have
loaned his car to someone that night and he
said, "I never loan my car to anyone."
```

Figure 5-18. How to quote a suspect's statements

```
I showed her the original photo display and
she pointed to photo number four which was
that of Mr. Willis and said, "I'm sure he's
the one."
```

Figure 5-19. Example of when and how to quote a witness (an exception)

Furthermore, quoting witnesses may only serve to provide defense attorneys with a vehicle for claiming that the witness is lying every time there is the slightest variance between the words used by the witness on the stand and the words spoken to and quoted by the interviewing officer in the narrative report.

One exception to the rule of not quoting witnesses is when an eyewitness makes an identification of a suspect from either a lineup or a photo display. It is important to quote the statement of identification the eyewitness made, as in Figure 5-19. That statement is usually admissible as an exception to the hearsay rule in most states, therefore, the officer will likely be able to testify to what the eyewitness said about the identification.

When interviewing suspects (or witnesses who overheard a suspect's statements), the words spoken by the suspect should be quoted, as in Figure 5-20.

```
I asked Mr. Hartness why he went to the trailer
park, and he said, "To see if I could find out
more about burning down businesses." I asked him
what he meant by that, and he smiled and said,
"You'll find out soon enough."
```

Figure 5-20. Quoting a suspect's words

This is because it is the officer or the witness, not the suspect, who will be called to the stand to testify to what the suspect said. In these cases it is far more important that the judge and jury hear precisely what the suspect said, rather than what the officer or witness understood the suspect to mean. It is the job of the judge and jury to decide what the suspect meant, not what the officer or witness thought the suspect meant.

Opinions and Conclusions

As a general rule it is best to avoid including opinions and conclusions in the narrative report. As with most general rules there are important exceptions. One obvious exception is the common practice of expressing an opinion about everyday matters such as speed, weight, size, distance, or material (cotton, iron, plastic, etc.).

An occasion when it is necessary to write an opinion or conclusion in the narrative report is when the officer's opinion or conclusion is not common but is due to special training and experience. In this case the opinion or conclusion should be included, but only when the officer explains the facts that led to the conclusion, as in Figure 5-21.

```
I examined the broken wood sash window to the
bathroom of the tavern and concluded that that
was the point of entry because I saw a ladder had
been placed against the wall at the window level
which was twelve feet from the ground.
Furthermore, the window had been broken out and
numerous glass fragments littered the floor
inside and very few glass fragments were on the
outside. I also noticed that the ground was wet
and that there were muddy shoe prints on the
floor leading from the window toward the interior
of the tavern.
```

Figure 5-21. Proper way to explain conclusions

```
Mr. Gessele invited me into his front room where
I saw a small child whom I later identified as
Julie Van Ranst, age seven. She appeared to be
very afraid of Mr. Gessele because she watched
him constantly, and when he walked over to her
and held out his hand, she began to cry and
crawled under the coffee table saying, "No, no,
no. You'll hurt me."
```

Figure 5-22. Proper way to explain conclusions regarding emotional states

Other opinions or conclusions that are acceptable if accompanied by some factual explanation in the narrative report concern emotional states (happy, sad, angry, hysterical, etc.), as in Figure 5-22. Since most people can readily recognize these common emotional states with a minimal explanation, the explanation by the officer should be rather short.

Writing out the factual basis for these types of opinions or conclusions is very helpful to the reader, who should then be able to reach the same opinion or conclusion. Writing out the factual basis is valuable to the officer as well. When the officer is called to the witness stand and asked about an opinion or conclusion in the report, the officer must be able to recall the facts that compelled that conclusion or opinion.

It is dangerous to offer opinions or conclusions in the narrative report when the matter is going to be subjected to further expert scrutiny because of its nature. Examples might be whether a small stain is blood, or if the wound to the victim is a bullet entrance or exit wound or was caused by a knife. Other examples might be whether a powder is cocaine or if a mark was made by a particular pry tool. In this type of opinion it is preferable for the officer to write that the spot "appeared to be" blood or that the wound "appeared to be" a bullet wound. The qualifying phrase "appeared to be" is accurate and merely describes the appearance of something but does not render an opinion or form a conclusion.

Photocopying Evidence

One of the purposes of writing the narrative report is to communicate as directly and as effectively as possible. One way to enhance the written narrative report is to attach to the report a photocopy of an important piece of physical evidence that was seized or created during the investigation.

The visual impact that a picture of an important piece of evidence has on the person reading the report is significant. It is well worth the little time and effort needed to make the photocopy in the first place.

For example, if a bindle of cocaine was seized, it is a simple matter to place that bindle on a photocopy machine, make a copy of it, and attach that copy to the narrative report. Similarly if a piece of rope used to tie up the kidnap victim is recovered, or if a pocket watch stolen in a robbery is removed from the suspect's pocket, or if a knife used to terrorize a kidnap victim is seized, each can easily be copied on a photocopy machine and the copy attached to the report, as in Figure 5-23.

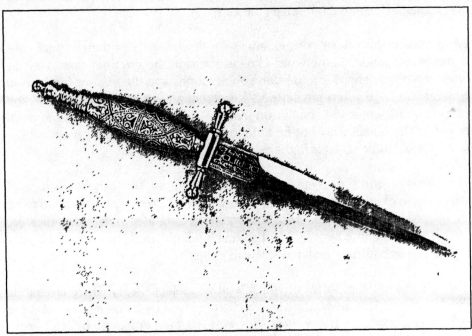

Figure 5-23. Photocopy of an item of evidence (knife)

SUMMARY

The choice of which words to use in the narrative report is completely up to the police officer writing the report. While the officer has choices, these choices have consequences. Some words, while clear, are awkward and stilted, whereas the same meaning can be conveyed with more commonly used words. The consequences are that, on the one hand, the officer appears stiff and awkward or with the more common word choice, at ease and comfortable.

Of course some words are not clear and might even create ambiguity. Some are general instead of specific; some are long and complicated instead of simple and direct. Some word choices are out of date and awkward, as in cases of officers who refer to themselves as "writer" or "undersigned" instead of the simple and direct "I."

There are some style choices that are far more dangerous when used in narrative police reports. One such dangerous choice is the use of the passive voice. "The gun was seized" describes a fact but does not communicate the most important thing about that fact—the name of the person who seized the gun. Without that person to testify that he or she seized the gun, it may likely be a useless fact because of the inability to prove it. Using the active voice solves the problem. "Deputy Dinh seized the gun."

Word choices also have consequences for the integrity of the criminal case under investigation. Some word choices damage the criminal case, such as when the officer chooses to describe observations and the reasons for them in general language when greater detail is essential. For example, suppose the officer simply writes the conclusion that the bathroom window was the point of entry. The officer may not be able to defend that conclusion months later since there will be no facts in the report to support it.

Thousands of words are available to the police officer. This can make chaos of the problem of which words to use, especially since so many words seem to be used interchangeably (e.g., said, told me, stated, related, inferred, indicated, etc.). The problem, however, is not so much which words to select but breaking writing habits that involve poor word choices.

The solution to the problem of which words to select is easy. There are only a handful of problem areas, most of which are solved by following some simple rules—i.e., shorter is better; write the way you talk; don't use police jargon. Other problem areas are solved by using common sense. For example, the officer must go into detail in the narrative report if likely to be asked for detail later on. (Why was the person frisked? Why was the bathroom window thought to be the point of entry?)

Those police officers who write narrative police reports command a powerful tool in the criminal justice system. This tool is most effective when the words chosen are designed to hit the mark cleanly and squarely.

▼ REVIEW QUESTIONS

1. What are the differences between active voice and passive voice? Why should passive voice be avoided in narrative police reports?
2. When should the past tense be used and when may the present tense be used in narrative police reports?
3. What are the correct ways of referring to adults and juveniles in narrative police reports?
4. Explain how to refer to unidentified people in narrative police reports.
5. Give three examples of police jargon and how they should be changed.
6. When should witnesses be quoted in narrative police reports?
7. Explain the statement that opinions and conclusions in narrative police reports are often dangerous. Explain how to eliminate the danger and improve the reports.

▼ WRITING DRILLS

1. Rewrite the following sentences to eliminate the passive voice. You will have to supply the actor.
    a) The car was searched.
    b) The house was kept under surveillance from 8:00 P.M. until 12:00 midnight.
    c) Mr. Struzar was brought to the scene of the traffic accident.
    d) The computer equipment was examined for possible latent prints.

2. For each of the following words or phrases, write a shorter, simpler word or phrase that means the same thing.

desisted	oral communication
abundance of	visually detected
accompanied by	vehicle
proceeded to	commenced foot pursuit
in opposition to	in proximity to
made communication with	made exit from

3. Change the following military times into A.M./P.M. times.

1437 hours	1221 hours
2101 hours	1900 hours
0600 hours	1158 hours
0909 hours	1816 hours
2400 hours	1527 hours
1330 hours	0100 hours

4. Pick out the single most identifiable, reasonably permanent characteristic about each of the following unidentified persons and insert that description into the following sentence:

I saw _____ run away from the crowd at the bus stop.

a) A boy in his late teens wearing a round earring in his left ear, a blue bandana over his head, and a black leather jacket with silver studs on the shoulders and arms.

b) A tall, thin, elderly man with a cane. He was bald except for a silver fringe of hair over his ears and he was wearing very thick glasses.

c) A woman in her thirties who had black hair pulled back into a bun. She wore a bright red, flowered dress with long sleeves and a lace collar.

d) An Hispanic adult male with a dark complexion and a pock-marked face. He had a thick handlebar mustache. He appeared to be in his fifties and wore cowboy boots.

5. Complete the following sentences by giving the reasons for the conclusions.

a) She appeared to be lying when she said she had never been in the barn because . . .

b) The little girl seemed to be very afraid of Mr. Mason because . . .

c) I concluded that the motorcycle had struck the right side of the Chevrolet because . . .

d) It appeared to me that the coins were the same ones stolen in the Butler burglary because . . .

CHAPTER SIX

▼

Diagrams

6.1 SKETCHING THE BASIC DIAGRAM

A narrative police report is often made clearer with the addition of a diagram sketched by the officer. The time and effort it takes to make a diagram are insignificant when compared to the benefit created. Diagrams communicate more information at a glance than do several paragraphs of descriptive language. Furthermore, diagrams reflect a great deal of care and professionalism on the part of the officer. In addition the fact that an officer had to examine the scene to be able to sketch the diagram makes it far more likely that more details about the scene will be remembered by the officer.

Diagrams have several uses in a criminal investigation. They document precise locations of objects at a scene. For example, taking exact measurements and diagramming roadways and intersections help describe how traffic collisions occurred. This chapter will explore three specialized uses: as a crime scene diagram (or a diagram to record an officer's observations at a particular scene), as a method of recording witnesses' statements, and as a method of documenting suspects' statements.

The basic diagram for each of these three specialized uses is sketched the same way, regardless of how it will be used. This allows an officer to learn only one method of sketching a diagram that is flexible enough for multiple uses. Several rules make drawing a diagram easier.

1. Divide the paper into two parts, one being one-third of the paper, the other being two-thirds. Sketch the diagram on the entire two-thirds portion, keeping the one-third portion for a legend. The legend is the key to understanding the meaning of the numbers or letters written on the diagram. The legend is an explanation of what each of the numbers or letters on the diagram means.
2. Write "N" for North on the top right of the diagram with an arrow pointed up to the "N." Always draw the diagram with North at the top of the page. Except for "N" and the letters or numbers for the legend, the only other writing that should be on the diagram portion is an address or other brief description of the area so that the reader will be able to recognize its location. This address or brief description should be written at the bottom of the diagram. At times it will be necessary to label a street on the diagram for clarity; but as a general rule nothing on the diagram should be labeled.
3. All features on the diagram are to be sketched freehand from an overhead perspective. The features should be sketched so that they look as much as possible like the actual object they are portraying as seen from overhead, as in Figure 6-1. Features that are to be represented by letters

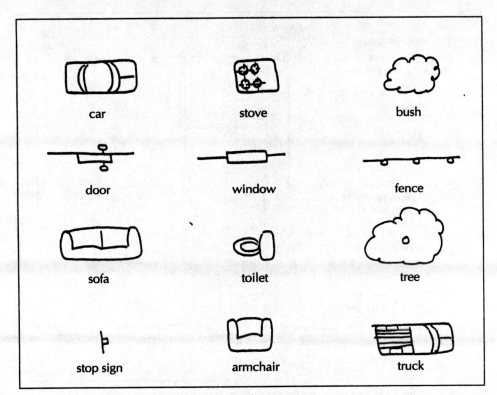

Figure 6-1. Drawn features in a diagram sketch

or numbers on the diagram and explained in the legend should not be drawn on the diagram.

4. Draw in only those objects that are relevant to the investigation.

5. Do not draw the diagram to scale, but keep the objects and areas in perspective. Draw sizes and shapes as near in proportion to the surrounding objects and areas as possible.

6. At times, an officer may wish to sketch a wall as part of the diagram to show that evidence was discovered there or that something happened on that vertical surface. This can be done by drawing the wall as if it literally had been separated from the roof and the other walls and laid down on the ground adjacent to the floor of the structure. Then the wall surface can be drawn in the same way as the floor was drawn, i.e., from an overhead perspective, as in Figure 6-2.

7. Diagrams may be of any place or of any object. For example, it is very common for officers to search automobiles and seize evidence from

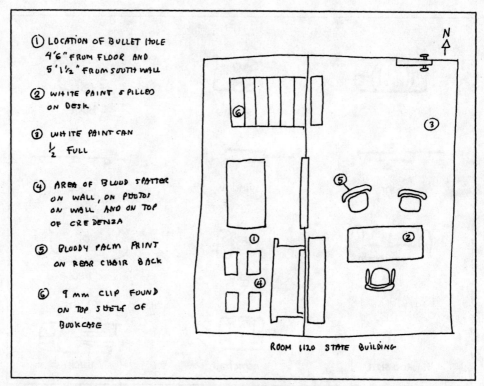

Figure 6-2. Overhead perspective with a wall in a diagram sketch

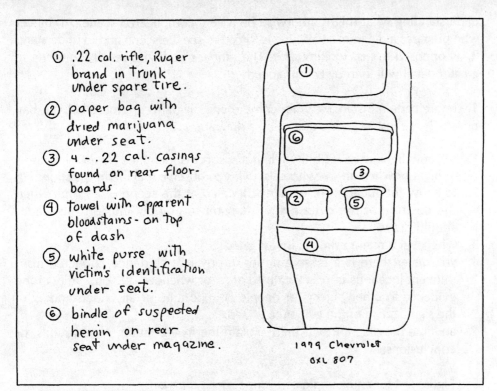

① .22 cal. rifle, Ruger brand in trunk under spare tire.

② paper bag with dried marijuana under seat.

③ 4 - .22 cal. casings found on rear floor-boards

④ towel with apparent bloodstains - on top of dash

⑤ white purse with victim's identification under seat.

⑥ bindle of suspected heroin on rear seat under magazine.

1979 Chevrolet
OXL 807

Figure 6-3. Diagram sketch of an automobile

various areas in and around automobiles. Diagrams are a very effective means of explaining where the evidence was found in the automobile, as in Figure 6-3.

6.2 DIAGRAMS FOR CRIME SCENES

An officer's report can be enhanced by the addition of a diagram to describe a crime scene or a scene where important observations were made or evidence was found. The purpose of such a diagram is to help the officer describe graphically where various items of evidence were found, and where marks, damage, scuffs, stains, and other similar conditions were seen. The officer may also use a diagram to show lighting sources and visibility. Such a diagram not only adds a professional touch to the report, it can be a significant help to the reader in understanding what might otherwise be a very complicated scene. An officer who prepares a diagram of a scene is forced to see the scene and to understand it, as opposed to just looking at it. The officer's ability to recall the scene in greater detail will thereby be enhanced.

There are certain instances when crime scene diagrams are more helpful than others. These instances include using a diagram

1. to show lighting or visibility when a suspect is identified by an eyewitness at night or when an eyewitness's ability to observe may be in question.
2. to show the location of evidence located at the scene of a crime when the position of the evidence is relevant to any conclusion the reader should draw.
3. whenever a major crime is investigated.
4. whenever there is a large amount of physical evidence collected from different locations in one localized area, or whenever the proximity of the evidence to other objects or people is important for an understanding of the significance of the evidence seized.
5. anytime the diagram will help explain the investigation, observations, or conclusions.

See Figure 6-4 for an example of a crime scene diagram.

6.3 DIAGRAMS TO RECORD WITNESSES' STATEMENTS

Written statements that are read, signed, and dated by witnesses serve many purposes. First, written statements allow the prosecution and the defense to evaluate the strengths and weaknesses of the case by learning exactly what the witnesses have to offer in the way of testimony. Second, such statements serve as an effective way for the person reading the report to be convinced that witnesses will say the same thing on the witness stand. Third, written statements are timeless in that they will always be there to refresh the witnesses' memory. If for some reason a witness is still unable to remember the event, the written statement itself may become the primary evidence under the "Past Memory Recorded" doctrine.

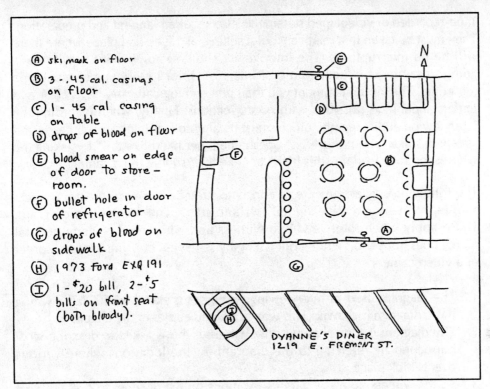

Figure 6-4. Diagram sketch of a crime scene

Despite the value of signed written statements, law enforcement officers usually only interview witnesses orally and then prepare a narrative report that incorporates what the witnesses told the officer. In important cases, signed written statements are obtained. It is unfortunate that signed written statements are not common. But because of the pressure of time that law enforcement officers face, it is understandable.

When a witness does give a signed written statement or a tape-recorded or videotaped statement, those types of statements are not only time-consuming, they must be prepared with some care in order for them to be useful. For example, written statements should be written out by the interviewing officer and shown to the witness, who then signs and dates the statement if it is accurate. It is rarely a good idea for a statement to be written out by a witness. There is no way to prevent the witness from including unnecessary, irrelevant, prejudicial, or embarrassing material, nor is there any way to ensure that the witness will include the necessary material.

Tape-recorded or videotaped statements also require planning and preparation. They must be taken in a relatively quiet setting, at a time and place where there will be no interruptions. The interviewer should know what the witness is going to say by conducting an oral interview prior to the tape or videotape recording. The taped statement will then proceed logically and be as clear and understandable as possible, with no corrections. Finally, when recording the interview on audiotape, the officer must be alert to clarifying any witness's oral statements like "about this high" or "she held her hand like this" by asking the witness to orally explain "this high" or "like this" so that the meaning is clear.

The following suggestions are intended to provide a way to create a quick, simple, but very effective signed "written statement" by using a diagram. These apply when interviewing a witness and when time or departmental policy does not permit writing out a lengthy statement or using a tape recorder or a video camera.

1. The diagram used in interviewing witnesses is sketched the same way a basic diagram is drawn. (This was explained earlier in the chapter.)
2. The diagram is then shown to the witness, who is asked to describe what happened by referring to the diagram for the locations where various events took place.
3. As the witness points to various locations on the diagram to explain what happened and where, the officer writes numbers or letters on the diagram where those activities took place.
4. The officer then writes a few short sentences or paragraphs in the legend section to describe what the witness said, using the same numbers or letters used on the diagram. The officer must be careful to use all of the numbers or letters that were used on the diagram when writing in the legend section. The officer need only then write a particular letter or number on the legend to describe where the event occurred.

Such diagrams are a simple way to enable a witness to describe a very complicated activity at a certain location. The diagram can be used to describe conduct, movement, statements made by people, and time sequences. Movement is best described on a diagram by drawing a line. Dotted, solid, or intermittent lines may be used to distinguish different people's movements. Once the line is drawn, the direction of travel can be shown by a single arrow placed in the middle of the line, as in Figure 6-5.

Statements may be reported simply by writing them in the legend section, using the same letter or number in the legend section as was used on the diagram to indicate where the person was when the statement was made, as in Figure 6-6.

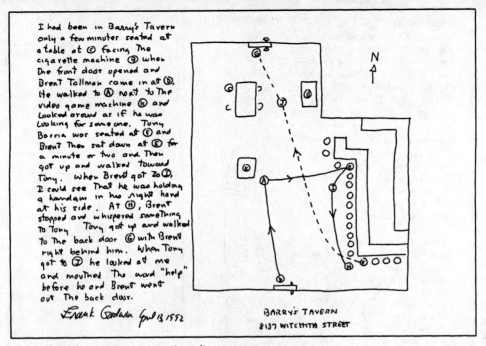

I had been in Barry's Tavern only a few minutes seated at a table at ⓒ facing the cigarette machine Ⓙ when the front door opened and Brent Tallman came in at Ⓓ. He walked to Ⓐ next to the video game machine Ⓚ and looked around as if he was looking for someone. Tony Borcia was seated at Ⓕ and Brent then sat down at Ⓔ for a minute or two and then got up and walked toward Tony. When Brent got to Ⓘ, I could see that he was holding a handgun in his right hand at his side. At Ⓗ, Brent stopped and whispered something to Tony. Tony got up and walked to the back door Ⓖ with Brent right behind him. When Tony got to Ⓘ he looked at me and mouthed the word "help" before he and Brent went out the back door.

Frank Cordova April 13, 1992

BARRY'S TAVERN
8137 WICHITA STREET

Figure 6-5. Showing movement in a diagram statement

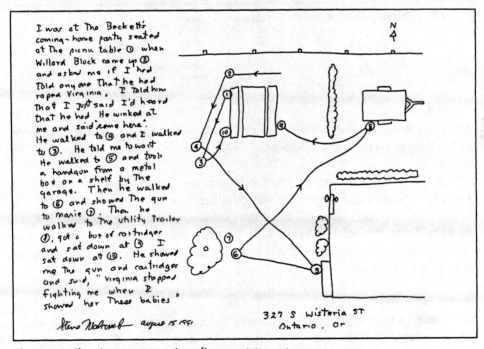

I was at the Beckett's coming-home party seated at the picnic table ① when Willard Block came up ② and asked me if I had told anyone that he had raped Virginia. I told him that I just said I'd heard that he had. He winked at me and said "come here". He walked to ④ and I walked to ③. He told me to wait. He walked to ⑤ and took a handgun from a metal box on a shelf by the garage. Then he walked to ⑥ and showed the gun to Marie ⑦. Then he walked to the utility trailer ⑧, got a box of cartridges and sat down at ⑨. I sat down at ⑩. He showed me the gun and cartridges and said, "Virginia stopped fighting me when I showed her these babies"

Steve Waltrowb august 15 1991

327 S Wisteria ST
Ontario, Or

Figure 6-6. Showing statements in a diagram statement

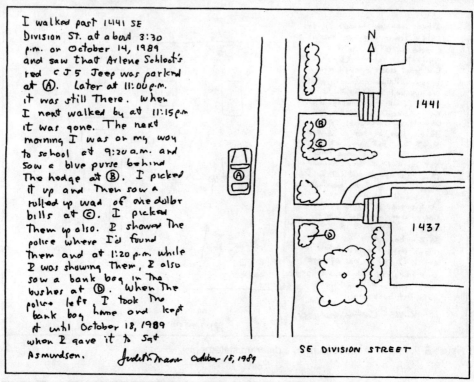

I walked past 1441 SE
Division St. at about 3:30
p.m. on October 14, 1989
and saw that Arlene Schloot's
red CJ5 Jeep was parked
at Ⓐ. Later at 11:00 p.m.
it was still there. When
I next walked by at 11:15 p.m
it was gone. The next
morning I was on my way
to school at 9:20 a.m. and
saw a blue purse behind
the hedge at Ⓑ. I picked
it up and then saw a
rolled up wad of one dollar
bills at Ⓒ. I picked
them up also. I showed the
police where I'd found
them and at 1:20 p.m. while
I was showing them, I also
saw a bank bag in the
bushes at Ⓓ. When the
police left, I took the
bank bag home and kept
it until October 18, 1989
when I gave it to Sgt
Asmundsen.
        Judith Mason October 15, 1989

SE DIVISION STREET

Figure 6-7. Showing time sequences in a diagram statement

Time sequences of when and where certain things occurred are also explained in the legend section, as in Figure 6-7.

When the officer finishes writing the legend section, the witness will read it over. If the witness agrees that the diagram and legend are accurate, the witness will sign and date it. If the witness also saw the suspect and is therefore an eyewitness, it would be valuable to have the witness write out a description of the suspect somewhere on the diagram in addition to signing and dating the diagram, as in Figure 6-8.

A diagram used to record a witness's statement is an effective means to refresh the witness's memory prior to testimony. Such diagrams are easy for witnesses to understand without having to read pages and pages of written material.

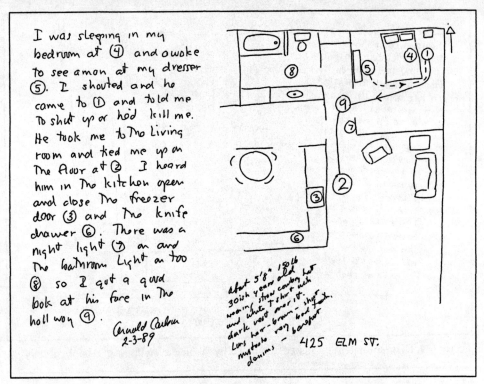

I was sleeping in my bedroom at ④ and awoke to see a man at my dresser ⑤. I shouted and he came to ① and told me to shut up or he'd kill me. He took me to the living room and tied me up on the floor at ② I heard him in the kitchen open and close the freezer door ③ and the knife drawer ⑥. There was a night light ⑦ on and the bathroom light on too ⑧ so I got a good look at his face in the hallway ⑨.

Arnold Carlson
2-3-89

about 5'8" 180 lb 30ish years old hat wearing straw cowboy hat and white T-shirt with dark vest over it. Luis hair brown - short mustache very long denims - barefoot

425 ELM ST.

Figure 6-8. Diagram statement signed and dated by an eyewitness, including a description of the suspect

Furthermore it is clear to the reader of the narrative report that the witness who signed the accompanying diagram more likely than not will be able to testify to a greater amount of detail confidently and accurately, regardless of how much time has passed.

Diagrams to record a witness's statement are easily and quickly prepared by the officer and take only a few minutes for the witness to complete with the officer's help.

In some cases where there are several eyewitnesses to the same event, using diagrams to interview all of the eyewitnesses may make the most sense. For example, in a bank robbery where there were several eyewitnesses, the diagram sketch of the interior of the bank would be photocopied, one for each

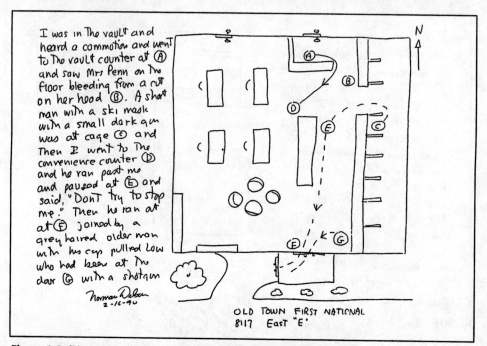

I was in The vault and heard a commotion and went to The vault counter at (A) and saw Mrs Penn on The floor bleeding from a cut on her head (B). A short man with a ski mask with a small dark gun was at cage (C) and Then I went to The convenience counter (D) and he ran past me and paused at (E) and said, "Don't try to stop me." Then he ran at at (F) joined by a grey haired older man with his cap pulled low who had been at The door (G) with a shotgun

Norman Dabcen
2-16-90

OLD TOWN FIRST NATIONAL
8117 East "E"

Figure 6-9. Diagram statement signed and dated by the first eyewitness to a bank robbery

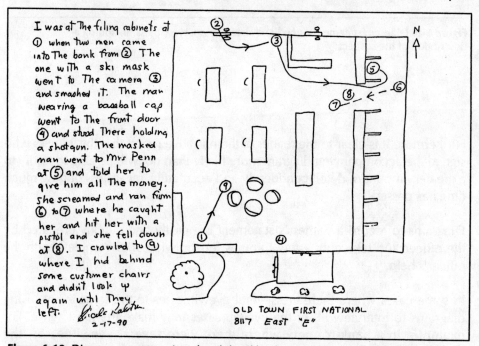

I was at The filing cabinets at (1) when two men came into The bank from (2) The one with a ski mask went to The camera (3) and smashed it. The man wearing a baseball cap went to The front door (4) and stood There holding a shotgun. The masked man went to Mrs Penn at (5) and told her to give him all The money. she screamed and ran from (6) to (7) where he caught her and hit her with a pistol and she fell down at (8). I crawled to (9) where I hid behind some customer chairs and didn't look up again until They left.

Gicale Rabretr
2-17-90

OLD TOWN FIRST NATIONAL
8117 East "E"

Figure 6-10. Diagram statement signed and dated by the second eyewitness to the same bank robbery as in Figure 6-9

eyewitness. The eyewitnesses would be interviewed one at a time by the officer. Eyewitnesses would point out on their own diagram their position and the position of the robbers during the robbery and what the robbers did and said during the robbery. If the robbers moved from one place to another during the robbery, that fact would also be pointed out on the diagram by the eyewitnesses.

See Figures 6-9 and 6-10 for examples of diagram statements from two different eyewitnesses to the same bank robbery.

6.4 DIAGRAMS TO RECORD SUSPECTS' STATEMENTS

The purposes of a criminal investigation are to identify the person(s) who committed the crime and to gather evidence that is admissible and proves facts with as much impact as possible. Oral statements made by suspects are given great weight by jurors and judges. Statements that are reduced to writing and signed by the suspect or that are tape-recorded have even greater impact at trial. The suspect has formally acknowledged the statement, and the physical evidence of the written or tape-recorded statement is an ever-present tangible reminder of the fact that the statement was made by the suspect.

While these types of physical evidence of a suspect's statement are very desirable, they are often difficult to obtain because of a suspect's natural reluctance to admit wrongdoing with such formality. The informality of merely talking about the case with an officer typically is not as threatening for the suspect. Tape-recorded and signed statements are to be sought after, but in the pursuit of these goals there is the simple and effective intermediate step of making use of a diagram during the conversation between the suspect and the officer. The diagram, when put to use during that conversation, becomes a piece of physical evidence that can be used at trial as an exhibit. It becomes a formal acknowledgment of wrongdoing by the suspect.

Diagrams can be used during an oral interview with a suspect in a very simple and informal fashion. For example, during the oral interview the officer should place a diagram in front of the suspect and ask the suspect to explain what happened by having the suspect point to areas on the diagram. After the suspect describes what was done by referring to the diagram, the officer will then have the suspect make a mark on the diagram to indicate where the suspect was when certain acts were performed. Next, the officer will write out a short phrase in the legend section to describe what the mark on the diagram means and then draw a line from that phrase to the mark on the diagram. After the officer writes the short phrase and draws a line to the mark, it is a simple matter to show the diagram and the phrase to the suspect and have the suspect acknowledge that they are accurate by initialing on the line to the mark and by dating and signing the diagram.

The number of marks made and phrases and lines drawn should be kept to a minimum. Often only two or three are all that are necessary.

This kind of diagram is easily prepared, is significantly less threatening to the suspect than is a tape recorder or video camera, and is very easy for the jury to understand.

See Figure 6-11 for an example of this type of diagram.

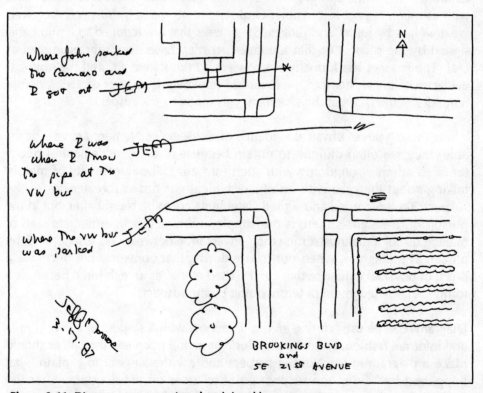

Figure 6-11. Diagram statement signed and dated by a suspect

SUMMARY

Sketched diagrams are one of the most underused aspects of police report writing. Police officers should be encouraged to use sketched diagrams as a simple, quick, and versatile tool that will enhance narrative reports, communicate facts more easily, and make it easier for witnesses to recall details.

Sketched diagrams are particularly oriented toward witnesses rather than reporting facts. Thus they complement the theme of this text that witnesses are more important than facts. For example, police officers prepare crime scene diagrams to enable them to recall greater detail more quickly when testifying. Also, police officers use diagrams in their interviews with suspects in order to be able to tell the judge or jury more clearly and convincingly what the suspect said. Other witnesses, too, rely on their diagram statements to refresh their memories with greater detail.

People who read the narrative report and the accompanying diagrams immediately gain two impressions: (1) the officer made an extra effort to create a more professional appearing report; (2) the facts are much more likely to be provable in court because of the close connection between the witnesses' statements and their obvious usefulness in court to ensure an accurate recollection.

For the small amount of time spent in preparing and using sketched diagrams, the dividends are many and the impact on the criminal case is substantial.

▼ REVIEW QUESTIONS

1. Explain the benefits of each type of diagram.
   a) Crime scene diagram
   b) Witness statement diagram
   c) Suspect interview diagram
2. What kind of writing should be found on the sketch section of a diagram?
3. Explain how to draw a vertical surface on the sketch, such as the wall of a room.
4. What type of writing is placed in the legend section of each of the three types of diagrams?
5. When showing movement of a person from one place to another on the sketched diagram, where is the arrow placed to indicate direction of movement?

▼ WRITING DRILLS

1. Draw the following objects freehand from an overhead perspective.
   a) van
   b) pickup truck
   c) car
   d) dresser
   e) bed
   f) house and detached garage
   g) fence
   h) hedge
   i) sliding glass door
   j) kitchen sink

2. Rewrite the following paragraph, omitting all references to locations. In their place, write letters to represent all locations as if writing the legend section of a diagram statement for a witness.

   I was standing next to the right front of my pickup when I saw Tom Sandler come out of his basement door. He walked over to the tire swing by the big maple and reached behind the tree next to the wooden fence, picked up a shotgun, and walked to the front door of Marshall Dixon's house. He fired the shotgun at the big plate glass window to the right of the front door and then ran back to his basement door, passing within ten feet of me. As he passed me, he looked at me and said, "I told him I'd get back at him."

CHAPTER SEVEN

▼

Eyewitness Interviews/ Photo Display Identification

7.1 THE NATURE OF EYEWITNESS EVIDENCE

The identification of persons who commit crimes is one of the most important goals of the police officer's investigation. One common method of identifying a suspect is through an eyewitness. An eyewitness is a person who saw the suspect at or near the crime scene or under other circumstances that connect the suspect to the commission of the crime.

When an eyewitness is first located, the officer must cover all of the critical areas of eyewitness identification during the interview with the eyewitness.

Later, when a suspect has been developed, the officer may mount a photograph of that suspect in a folder, along with several photographs of people who are similar in appearance to the suspect. The officer's next step is to show the photo display to the eyewitness to see if the eyewitness can identify the suspect. If an identification is made by the eyewitness, that fact is ordinarily a very important piece of evidence in the later prosecution.

Defense attorneys are routinely vigorous in their cross-examinations of eyewitnesses who have made identifications from photo displays. Some psychologists have even testified as expert witnesses that eyewitness identification is almost always unreliable under most circumstances. Courts, too, are questioning eyewitness identifications and the photo display process more and more. However, since the preparation of the photo display and the showing of the display to the eyewitness are both wholly within the control of the investigating officer, there is little reason why this procedure cannot be fair, the evidence admissible in court, and the testimony convincing to the jury.

This chapter will show how to write the narrative report of an interview with an eyewitness and what areas must be covered during that interview. It is important that not only certain questions be asked, but that the narrative report reflect the questions and the answers. This chapter will also cover the preparation of a proper photo display, how to show it to an eyewitness, and how that procedure should be written in the narrative report.

It is important to conduct the interview/identification process correctly. It is also important to write the narrative report in a way that clearly shows the fairness and effectiveness of both the interview process and the identification process.

7.2 INTERVIEWING
THE EYEWITNESS

The identification process begins with the initial interview of the eyewitness. This initial interview is every bit as important as the later interview during which the eyewitness is shown the photo display. Each initial eyewitness interview must follow the same pattern because there are elements that must be addressed by the officer in every such interview.

1. The officer should get a detailed description of what the eyewitness saw and heard. For example, in discussing the suspect's hair, it is good to ask the eyewitness to be specific about details such as length, color, part, curliness, combed, unkempt, etc. The report documents what the eyewitness recalls.
2. The officer also needs to report the factors that affected the eyewitness's ability to observe the suspect (length of time, lighting, distance, speed, etc.). Especially important are the unusual or startling events that caused the eyewitness's attention to be drawn to the suspect.

3. Eyewitnesses need as much help as possible to be able to recall the details of what they saw of the suspect. It is not sufficient for the officer simply to write what the eyewitness said. The officer must do something more that will help the eyewitness recall the description at the trial of the case. A simple way to help the eyewitness later recall the suspect's description is for the officer to prepare a "memory aid device." This is simply a scrap of paper on which the eyewitness jots down the description of the suspect and then dates and signs the scrap of paper, as in Figure 7-1. An alternative method is to have the eyewitness write the description on the diagram used to take the eyewitness's statement. (See Figure 6-8.)

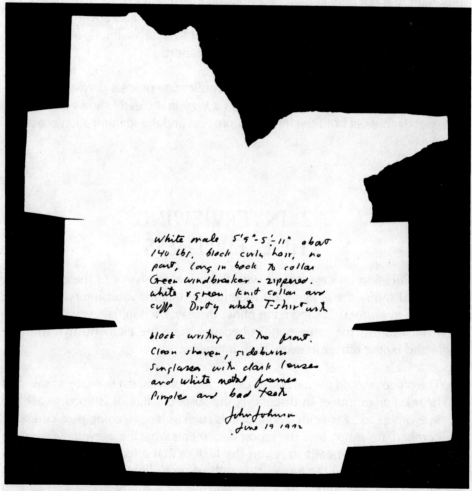

Figure 7-1. An eyewitness's memory aid device

4. The officer should always ask if the eyewitness will be able to recognize the person again.
5. It is important that the officer remember to interview multiple eyewitnesses separately. Eliminate any chance for a claim to be made that one eyewitness's memory was colored by what other eyewitnesses said.

7.3 REPORTING THE EYEWITNESS INTERVIEW

When reporting the initial eyewitness interview, the same rules for reporting any witness's statement still apply. The <u>ACTION TAKEN</u> section will contain a brief reference to the fact of the interview and to any physical evidence created during the interview, such as a diagram statement or a memory aid device made by the eyewitness.

In addition, however, the <u>STATEMENTS</u> section must contain (1) the detailed description of the suspect, (2) the information about the eyewitness's ability to observe, and (3) the question—and the answer—about the eyewitness being able to recognize the person again, as in Figure 7-2.

7.4 PREPARING THE PHOTO DISPLAY

The preparation of the photo display is under the control of the investigating officer. The display must be fair and must appear to be fair. It must also be retained permanently as a piece of evidence. If necessary, it should be possible to re-create it in the event it is disassembled and the individual photos replaced in the agency's files. It is usually advisable to mount the photos in a file folder permanently, and thereafter treat the photo display as any other piece of physical evidence. The steps for preparing a typical photo display:

(Excerpt from <u>ACTION TAKEN</u>):

I interviewed Mr. Kennedy in his living room as
he was being given first aid by the ambulance
attendants. He gave me a description of the man
who robbed him. He also wrote out the description
on a piece of paper and dated and signed it.

(Excerpt from <u>STATEMENTS</u>):

Mr. Kennedy told me that the man who robbed him
was a white male in his early twenties, was
about six feet tall, and weighed about 160 lbs.
The man had a black ski mask over his head and a
red T-shirt and a denim jacket with a white
fleece collar. The man had a white birthmark on
his lower lip.

Mr. Kennedy said that the robbery took place
under a streetlight and that he had a clear look
at the man. Also, the man told him, "I'm really
sorry but I've got to have a fix."

Mr. Kennedy told me that he thought he would be
able to recognize the man if he saw him again.

Figure 7-2. How to report the eyewitness interview

1. Mount the pictures permanently in a file folder and keep the display as evidence. Use at least six different photographs for the photo display.
2. Use photographs of persons similar in age, appearance, hair length, style, etc.
3. Have the same or similar appearing background in each photograph.
4. Do not allow the date of the photographs to appear visible.
5. Do not allow the height marks in the background to appear visible.
6. Number the photos on the original photo display.

An example of how a typical photo display would look is shown in Figure 7-3.

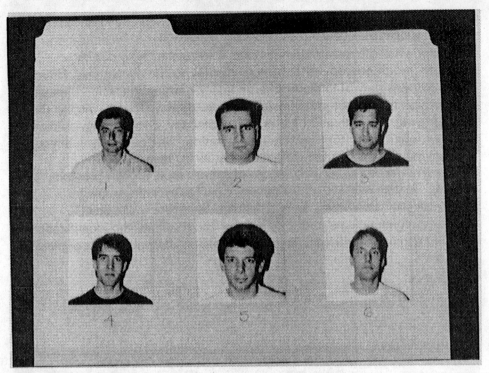

Figure 7-3. An example of a photo display

7.5 SHOWING THE PHOTO DISPLAY

Showing the photo display to the eyewitness is a very sensitive point in the investigation of a criminal case. A mistake here can cause the eyewitness's future identification testimony to be questioned, if not suppressed. The officer must avoid pitfalls and do whatever is necessary to make the process not only fair but convincing. The necessary steps are:

1. Take the original photo display file folder to the interview, along with a photocopy of the photo display.
2. Repeat the following or similar words to the eyewitness: "I am going to show you some photographs of people. The person you saw may or may not be among these photographs. Please look at them carefully and tell me if you recognize any of them."

3. Next, show the display to the eyewitness and discreetly make note of the time it takes the eyewitness to make or fail to make an identification.
4. Report what the eyewitness says after viewing the photo display.
5. Show the photocopy of the photo display to the eyewitness. Have the eyewitness draw a circle on the photocopy around the same photograph that was picked out on the original photo display. The eyewitness should then write the date and time on the photocopy, as well as an estimate of how long it took to make the identification. Finally, the eyewitness will sign the photocopy of the photo display, as in Figure 7-4.
6. Never write on the original photo display. It must be kept preserved in its original state so that the jury can see what the eyewitness saw.
7. Never show the display to more than one eyewitness at a time.
8. Never communicate to the eyewitness the results of the identification or failure to make an identification by expressing disappointment or pleasure.

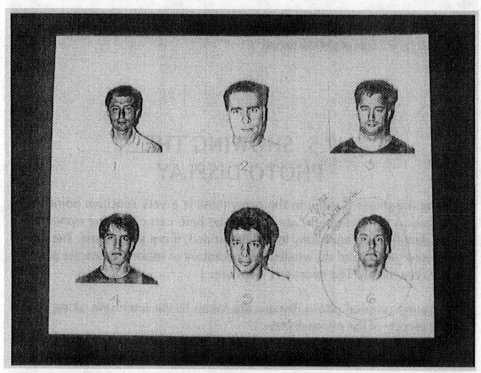

Figure 7-4. A photocopy of the photo display signed by an eyewitness, who also writes the date, the time, and the estimated time it took to make the identification

When showing the photo display, the officer should discreetly note the actual amount of time it took the eyewitness to make the identification. Shortly thereafter, the officer should have the eyewitness make an estimate of the same time. The purpose of the officer noting the time discreetly is to keep the eyewitness from feeling pressured. This still allows the officer to testify to the precise amount of time. The purpose of the eyewitness making an estimate is so it can be written on the photocopy of the photo display, which will refresh the eyewitness's memory at a later time. These two times—one an actual time, one an estimated time—are likely to be slightly different.

An identification that actually took a few seconds may well turn into a matter of minutes in the eyewitness's own mind months later. It is important to give the eyewitness the ability to testify confidently and accurately about which photo was identified, the date and time the identification was made, as well as the amount of time it took.

7.6 REPORTING THE PHOTO DISPLAY SHOWING

When reporting the eyewitness's photo display interview, the same rules for any witness's statement apply. In <u>ACTION TAKEN</u>, the officer will report that a photo display interview was conducted, the actual amount of time taken by the eyewitness to make the identification, and any physical evidence created or used during the process. Such evidence includes the eyewitness viewing the original photo display plus the eyewitness writing on and signing the photocopy of the photo display.

Eyewitness photo display interview information is to be included in the <u>STATEMENTS</u> section of the narrative. It directly explains and enhances the statement of identification made by the eyewitness. The information to be written in the <u>STATEMENTS</u> section will include the cautionary statements made to the eyewitness (e.g., "I am going to show you . . . ," etc.), the showing of the photo display, the eyewitness's response, and the eyewitness's own estimate of the amount of time it took to make the identification.

See Figure 7-5 for narrative report examples of how to report a photo display interview with an eyewitness.

> I met Mr. McMurray at his gas station at about
> 7:35 P.M. and showed him the photo display. He
> picked the picture of Mr. Thomas Darensburgh in
> exactly twelve seconds. I then handed him a
> photocopy of the photo display and had him
> circle Mr. Darensburgh's photograph, date and
> sign it and write on it his estimate of the
> number of seconds it took him to make the
> identification.

(Excerpt from <u>STATEMENTS</u>):

> I told Mr. McMurray that I was going to show him
> some photographs of people and that the person
> who robbed him may or may not be among the
> photographs but to look at them carefully and
> tell me if he recognized anyone.
>
> Mr. McMurray looked at the photographs and
> pointed to photograph number five and said,
> "That's the man. I'll never forget his face." Mr.
> McMurray estimated that it took him twenty
> seconds to make the identification.

Figure 7-5. How to report the photo display showing and the interview

SUMMARY

Of all witnesses, the eyewitness is the most vulnerable to attacks by defense attorneys bent on showing that the judge or jury should not base their decision on the eyewitness's testimony. In a jury's eyes, the eyewitness is often the key to whether or not the defendant is the one who committed the crime. If they believe the eyewitness, the defendant is usually convicted. If they doubt the eyewitness, the defendant is usually acquitted.

Unfortunately for law enforcement, eyewitnesses are typically civilians who have had little or no experience with the criminal justice system or as witnesses. They are almost always ill at ease on the witness stand and uncomfortable with cross-examination. They are likely to rise to a defense attorney's bait, lose composure, and answer in anger. They are often the weakest link in the state's case. On the other hand, they can be the strongest part of the state's case.

Fortunately for law enforcement, the cases involving eyewitnesses can be investigated and the reports written in such a way that the eyewitness becomes one of the strongest factors in the case. The way to do this centers on the idea that eyewitnesses need help in accurately recalling facts so that their testimony comes from refreshed memory and is presented with confidence. A corollary to this is the idea that the narrative report must be written so that the strength of the eyewitness's testimony against the suspect is clear and convincing.

Interviews with eyewitnesses are a critical stage of an investigation. The officer must be sure to get detailed descriptions, identify factors bearing on an eyewitness's ability to observe, and find a way to preserve the event for the eyewitness's later recall. The officer must then write a narrative report that covers each of these areas.

▼ REVIEW QUESTIONS

1. In which section of the narrative report is the eyewitness's description of the suspect written?
2. What is a memory aid device and why is it included in the <u>ACTION TAKEN</u> and <u>EVIDENCE</u> sections?
3. In which section of the narrative report do you find this question to the eyewitness: "Do you think you will be able to recognize this person if you see this person again?"
4. Explain how to prepare a photo display. How do you ensure that it can be preserved for use at a future trial?
5. What three statements are made to the eyewitness just before the eyewitness is shown a photo display?
6. Why is it necessary to keep track of the actual amount of time the eyewitness took to make an identification?
7. Why should you ask for the eyewitness's own best estimate of the amount of time taken to make an identification?
8. What does the eyewitness write on the photocopy of the photo display after an identification is made from the original of that photo display?
9. Why do you think you should never tell any eyewitness the results of the identification process?

▼ WRITING DRILLS

1. Using only the important facts from the following information, write a proper paragraph for <u>STATEMENTS</u>, demonstrating how to write about an interview with an eyewitness.

   During your interview with Mildred Dosset, she told you that she saw a man walking between her trailer and her neighbor's trailer. The interview took place on April 7, 19—, at 4:15 P.M. in Mrs. Dosset's living room at her home, 14471 SE Wildwood, space 27A, Hampton. There was a very bright yard light that lit up the area. He was going toward the woods at the rear of their properties. Mrs. Dosset said she could see that the man was in his fifties, wearing a blue jacket and black pants. He also wore white tennis shoes. It was late at night and very unusual for anyone to be going to the woods at that hour. She thought she could recognize him if she saw him again. Mrs. Dosset thought it was very unusual for anyone to be where the man was, because no one ever uses that way to get to the woods. A person would have to climb over two fences to do so. She said that the man wore dark glasses and needed a shave. His eyebrows were very bushy. He was of average height and build.

2. Using only the important facts from the information provided in the previous writing drill, write a proper paragraph for <u>ACTION TAKEN</u>, demonstrating how to refer to an interview with an eyewitness.

▼ NOTES

CHAPTER EIGHT

▼

The Police Field Notebook

8.1 AS A TOOL

The police officer's field notebook is a tool of the profession, as are the officer's gun, handcuffs, and car radio. The field notebook is a very personal tool that is made useful to the officer by what is written in it. It performs several different functions important to the officer personally and to police work as a whole. These functions will be covered in this chapter.

The notebook, when properly filled in, becomes a source of information for the officer about things that happened or things the officer noticed during each shift. Accurate information is very important to efficient police work. It usually determines the priority attached to various cases or activities. The information in the notebook allows the officer to recall facts for later reports and to explain to others what happened during the officer's shift.

8.2 AS A COLLECTION OF INFORMATION

The notebook serves as an important source of information necessary to all police work. For example, the officer may write down the names and

```
2:12 am              ped conv.

2 WMA dk clothes  EB E Clover ST
N side  w of RR Trax carr. large
green chest betw. Them. Stopped
turned watched me as I drove
past. Trnd-stop-They walked up.
    (1) DON NMI GILSTROP 06-11-59
      2622 E. faraday St
      Monroe Idaho 96212
    (2) BENJAMIN CARL DAY  11-17-62
      141 SE Hwy 41
      Medford  OR


Chest = green w/ black trim - rope
handles - SILVER PADLOCK-HASP RUSTY
4' x 3' x 3'.
GILSTROP - belongs to gf. SANDI
CONNOR - moving it to her new
house 3 more blocks E. Clover.
```

Figure 8-1. Using the field notebook to record suspicious circumstances

addresses of people found in unusual or suspicious circumstances, as well as a brief explanation of those circumstances, as in Figure 8-1. The officer might also record things that experience suggests are so unusual as likely to be related to criminal activity, such as a strange car parked too long in a place where it appears to have no legitimate reason to be. Hours, days, or even weeks later this information may prove to be of critical importance.

Correct spelling is vitally important, as are accurate dates, times, dates of birth, descriptions, and measurements. The officer must make every effort to record only the most accurate of information in the notebook if it is to be of maximum benefit.

8.3 AS NOTES FOR
A LATER REPORT

The police field notebook serves as a place for the officer to write down factual information until later, when it is reviewed for the purpose of writing the report.

It is a place for the officer to capture the information needed for incorporation into the report. Writing the times of dispatch and arrival along with any additional information given out by the dispatcher is a typical way to begin notes that may be used in writing a later report, as in Figure 8-2. The officer will then

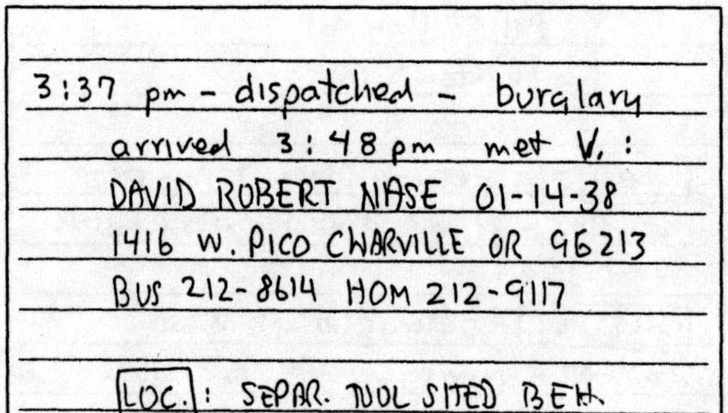

3:37 pm - dispatched - burglary
arrived 3:48 pm met V, :
DAVID ROBERT NASE 01-14-38
1416 W. PICO CHARVILLE OR 96213
BUS 212-8614 HOM 212-9117

LOC.: SEPAR. TOOL SHED BEH.
GAR. - ABOVE DOD. - FORCED HASP.

V. ARR. HOM. 1:55 pm to find
LATE 70's dk blue 4 dr chev
poor faded paint, torn seat cvrs,
in d/way. WMA both wheel
+ started veh + sped off.
DESC: early 20's black curly
hair - gold bead earring
in left ear. clean shaven
dirty blue windbreaker -
white striped knit collar.

Figure 8-2. Using the field notebook to record burglary notes for a later report

note exact names, addresses, phone numbers, and dates of birth of any persons interviewed. Information provided by witnesses as to what they saw and heard may be written in the notebook in an abbreviated fashion.

Often the police officer will have facesheet forms on which the report can be written. Sometimes, in very simple cases where no narrative is necessary, the officer may write the entire report directly on the forms without making any extensive field notebook entries. In those cases, only the simplest information will be put in the notebook: names, addresses, dates of birth, the report case number, and a brief explanation of the event.

Of course not every call a police officer responds to will result in a later report, but each should result in at least a notebook entry being made. For example, if dispatched to a call of a prowler but unable to locate anyone, the officer will usually only log in the notebook the time of the call and the name, address, and date of birth of the citizen who complained, plus a description of the prowler and the circumstances. The time the officer cleared the call will also be recorded in the notebook. Ordinarily there will be no formal written report about this incident, but there is always a possibility that the information will become important and that a report will have to be written later.

8.4 AS A PROTECTION AGAINST FALSE CLAIMS

By documenting the correct factual information, the officer can use the field notebook to defend against false claims and accusations, as in Figure 8-3. For example, at the beginning of each shift, a prudent officer will record the assigned patrol car's number and mileage, as well as the condition of both the car and accompanying equipment, such as shotgun, camera, and radar gun. Should anyone wish to know whether the officer had a particular piece of equipment on a certain shift, the officer will be able to confirm or deny this by referring to the appropriate field notebook entry.

```
7-21-88
  4:50 pm                    10-8
  veh 1042                   72,042
  rider                      res. Warren
  patrol                     dist 3
  weather                    cloudy, dry
 NOTE    CRACKED RR WNDOW;
 W-W ARC SCAR ON RT SIDE FRNT
 WNDOW; 10" SCRAPE RR FENDER


  5:56 pm          motorist aid
 WFA alone waived dn - stalled
 10 MIN AFO - DES. RIDE TO
 GAS STA 47? - HWY 216.
          MONICA JEAN BAKER
          9227 MUNROE LANE
          BEAVERTON OR 97122
          06-11-49
 BEGIN     72,081.2    5:59 pm
 END       72,084.8    6:03 pm
```

Figure 8-3. Using the field notebook as a protection against false claims and accusations

The officer will record the beginning and ending times and mileage whenever a ride is given to a stranded motorist. Likewise the officer should also check the rear seat cage area of the patrol car at the beginning of each shift to make sure that it is clear, and then check it again after transporting anyone. If, after driving an arrested suspect to jail, the back seat is checked and a bindle of heroin is found, the officer will be able to testify that the heroin was not there before the suspect was put in the rear cage area of the patrol car.

A police officer quickly learns self-protection techniques under all circumstances. Much of an officer's training is directed toward that end (weapons training, self-defense, baton training, protective apparel such as rubber gloves, protective vest, etc.). The police field notebook also serves as such a tool by protecting the officer against false claims.

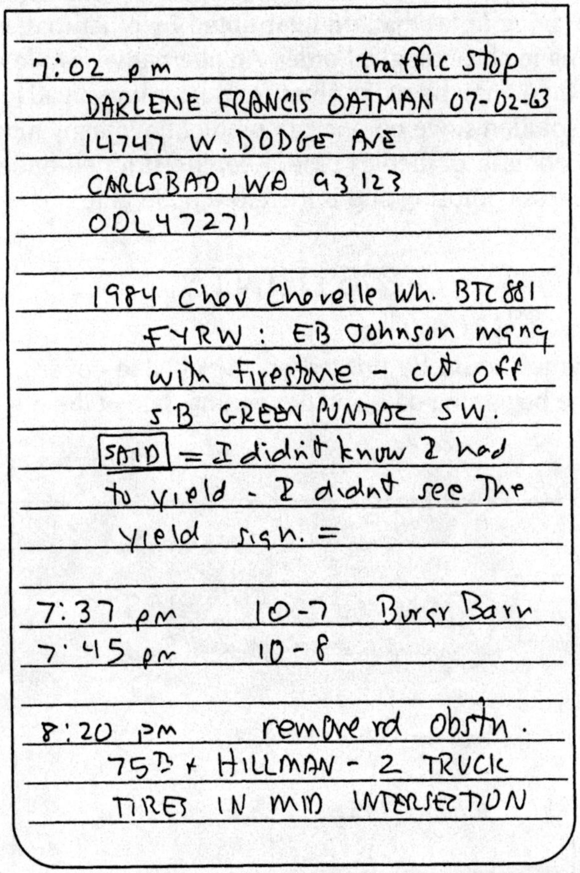
7:02 pm traffic stop
DARLENE FRANCIS OATMAN 07-02-63
14747 W. DODGE AVE
CARLSBAD, WA 93123
ODL47271

1984 Chev Chevelle Wh. BTC881
FYRW: EB Johnson mgng
with Firestone - cut off
SB GREEN PUNTIAC SW.
SAID = I didn't know I had
to yield - I didnt see The
yield sign. =

7:37 pm 10-7 Burgr Barn
7:45 pm 10-8

8:20 pm removed rd obstn.
75th + HILLMAN - 2 TRUCK
TIRES IN MID INTERSECTION

Figure 8-4. Using the field notebook as a log of activities

8.5 AS A LOG

One of the functions of the police field notebook is to record events and circumstances that happened during the officer's shift. In effect it is a log of the officer's activities in chronological order, as in Figure 8-4. Not everything an officer does during the shift is later written into a police report. In fact most activities during each shift never are the subject of a written report. For this reason the field notebook becomes the primary source of documentation of an officer's activities and observations while working a shift.

Notes in the field notebook make the most sense when they are written in chronological order prefaced always by the time of day. This may mean that a particular investigation that covered several days will be written in the officer's field notebook in such a way that it is interrupted by other notes about unrelated matters. Having notes that are interrupted by other matters is the consequence of writing in chronological order. An alternative is to leave blank pages at areas where there may be more notes from later investigative activities. This is an awkward solution since no one can predict how many more notes, if any, will be written about a particular case. Keeping strict chronological order in the notebook is less confusing and is therefore preferable.

8.6 HINTS

A Permanent Record

The officer's name should be printed on the outside cover of the notebook, together with the beginning date and the ending date of the notes contained in

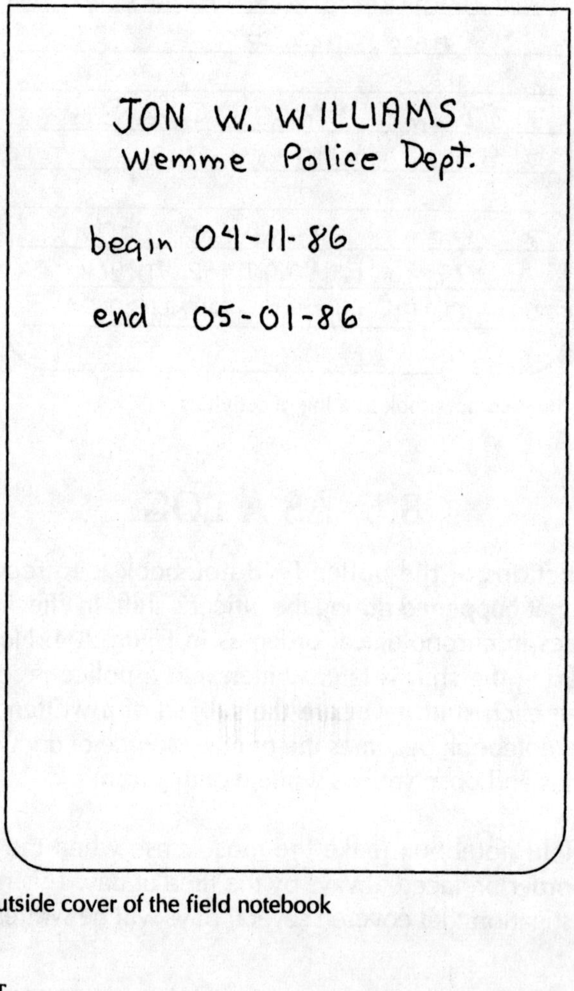

Figure 8-5. The outside cover of the field notebook

the notebook, as in Figure 8-5. These dates will help the officer find the proper notebook quickly among the other notebooks the officer has filled up and stored away. The officer should always write legibly and in ink; writing done in pencil can fade and can be smudged or erased.

Inside Cover
The inside cover is a convenient place for an officer to write down commonly used reference information, as in Figure 8-6. It typically contains a calendar and might also include such information as phone numbers frequently called, radio call codes, Miranda warnings, as well as the days and times the local court wants traffic offenders cited to appear.

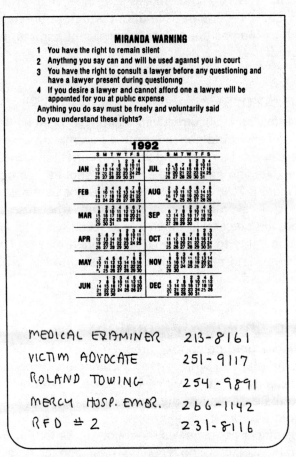

Figure 8-6. The inside cover of the field notebook

Permanent Pages

The type of notebook used by the officer should be one with permanently bound pages, not one with easily removed pages such as a loose-leaf notebook. Never tear pages out. Missing pages may be a source of confusion for the officer and a fertile ground for cross-examination by the defense attorney.

Language to Use

Since officers' notes are to be used for their own purposes, it is very common for officers to use symbols and shorthand in their notebooks. Writing in sentences is impractical. Officers commonly use radio call codes as a shorthand. For example, an officer going out for lunch at 1:30 P.M. may write, "1:30 P.M.—10-7—Burger Barn." When finished at 2:12 P.M., the officer may write, "2:12 P.M.—10-8." The 10-7 code means "out of service" and the 10-8 code means "in service." There is no rule about which abbreviations or words should be used, as long as the officer is consistent and can understand the abbreviations used.

Correcting Errors

If an officer finds that some incorrect information has been written down in the notebook, the officer should go back to that information, draw a single line through it (so it can still be read), and write the correct information just above or below it. The date and time of the correction should then be written in the margin, as in Figure 8-7. It is a poor idea to erase or obliterate any writing in the field notebook—even if it is being corrected—because it is likely that, once obliterated, the officer will be unable to recall what the error was in the first place. This inability to recall what was written may be confusing to the officer who testifies and may provide a defense attorney with a chance to embarrass or criticize the officer.

Personal Comments or Opinions

The police officer's field notebook, although a very individualized tool for each officer, is no place to write personal comments or opinions. On some occasions the defendant's attorney may be allowed to examine the field notes with respect to the case against the defendant. This is especially true if the notes in the field notebook are the only information the officer has on the subject, or if the officer has reviewed those notes prior to trial. For example, in typical minor traffic violations, no report is written and the notebook is the sole

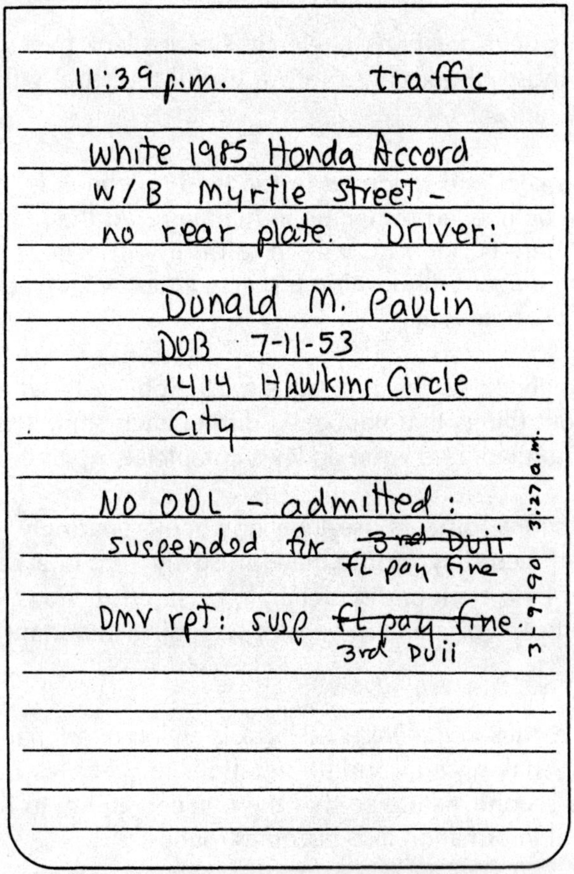

Figure 8-7. How to correct an error in the field notebook

source of the officer's recollection. In such cases the defense attorney and the defendant may very well have the right to inspect the officer's notes regarding that particular case.

Care should be exercised regarding what is written. An officer's personal opinion as to the quality of the case and the character of witnesses, suspects, or victims should never be written in the notebook. Should any embarrassing comments or opinions exist in the notebook, the police officer may have to explain them under cross-examination.

SUMMARY

A police officer's field notebook begins its life as blank pages. It is up to the officer to turn those blank pages into a useful tool that will serve several purposes for the officer.

The information kept and recorded in the field notebook is information that may or may not be needed sometime in the future. At the time information is being written, there is often no way to tell if it will ever be needed again. Therefore a wise officer will develop a policy about what type of information to enter in the field notebook.

Primarily the notebook serves as a place for the officer to write down factual information about things that happened during each shift. The choice about what kinds of information to write down is completely up to the officer.

In some jurisdictions, officers use their notebooks sparingly — for example, where a detailed recording of information usually kept in a notebook is kept electronically or by a clerk or dispatcher. In most jurisdictions, however, notebooks are an officer's principal means of recording important information in the field.

Making regular entries in the field notebook is an important part of the officer's routine activity. Making appropriate notations and entries in the notebook should become second nature so that the officer's ability to refresh memory and recall factual information also becomes routine.

▼ REVIEW QUESTIONS

1. List at least four separate purposes served by a police field notebook.
2. Is it permissible in the field notebook for an officer to use abbreviations? cryptic phrases or words? personal opinions? Explain why or why not.
3. How can a police field notebook serve as a protection against false claims and accusations?
4. What kind of information is typically written on the inside front cover of a field notebook?
5. Explain how to best correct errors found in the police field notebook.

▼ NOTES

▼

CHAPTER NINE

How to Testify in Court

9.1 PREPARING TO TESTIFY

Read the Report

Upon being subpoenaed to testify in court, and prior to the day of trial, a police officer should read both the facesheet and the narrative report of that incident. The officer should also examine the physical evidence, including all photographs, diagrams, etc. The report should be read with the same critical eye for detail and comprehension that the defense attorney will use. The defense attorney will have carefully read the report to fashion cross-examination questions for the officer. The officer must prepare for that cross-examination by reading the report just as carefully.

If there are any inconsistencies, conclusions without supporting facts, unexplained conduct on the part of the officer, or items omitted in the officer's narrative report, cross-examination will ferret those out at the officer's expense. The defense attorney might even get the officer angry, frustrated, or petulant on the stand, thereby making the officer appear incompetent and the testimony seem confused or not credible.

The officer will meet with the prosecutor to discuss the case prior to trial. If the officer has discovered any problems or errors in the report, the officer must be sure to discuss these with the prosecutor as soon as possible before the trial. Most prosecutors, if they know of the problem prior to trial, are able to deal with it in such a way that the problem is either eliminated or the sting taken from it at the trial. It is only when the prosecutor is unaware of the problem that it may cause major difficulties for the officer and for the case.

Bring the Report

On the day of trial, the officer must bring a clean copy of the report to the trial. Leave the coffee-stained, dog-eared copy at the police station. The officer will also need a fresh file folder in which to place the police report. The file folder containing the report should be carried in the officer's left hand upon approaching the witness stand. The jury will be aware that the officer is carrying an important packet of papers to the stand. They may not know what is in the file folder, but they will assume it is related to the case at hand in some important way because the papers are being treated so carefully.

Pulling a folded and creased police report out of a pocket while on the stand reduces the apparent significance and importance of that report.

9.2 APPROACHING THE STAND: BEING SWORN

As the police officer approaches the witness stand with the reports in the file folder, the officer should be aware from previous experience or from watching others testify in the courtroom that witnesses are sworn in by a single court official, usually a clerk or a bailiff. The court official will typically allow the witness to walk toward the witness stand, but at some point the official will approach the witness and ask the witness to pause and raise his or her right hand. At that point, the official will swear in the witness.

The police officer should walk confidently toward the witness stand, halt, and face the clerk with right hand raised at or before the spot where witnesses are usually sworn in. If the officer can do this without having been told to do so by the clerk, the impact on those watching is clear: the officer is an experienced witness.

9.3 ON THE WITNESS STAND:
HOW TO USE THE REPORT

The reports in the file folder should rest unopened on the officer's lap during testimony until the officer is directed to read them or until the officer needs them for refreshing memory on a particular point before answering a question. In either event it is important that the officer take this opportunity to let the jury know what the documents in the file folder are.

If the prosecutor is also interested in enlightening the jury, the questions by the prosecutor and the officer's answers might appear as in Figure 9-1.

Q: Officer Kennedy, please tell the jury exactly what Mrs. Whitlock's words were.
A: May I refresh my memory by looking at my report?
Q: Is that your report in the folder you took to the stand with you?
A: Yes.
Q: When did you write that report?
A: The same night that Mr. Opheim was injured and shortly after I finished my investigation.
Q: Do you regularly write police reports in your job?
A: Yes.
Q: Have you had any training in writing police reports?
A: Yes, I've had eight hours of classroom training as well as in-service training at roll call on an on-going basis every year. I also have my reports reviewed by the duty sergeant every time they are written.
Q: Why do you write reports, Officer?
A: So that I will be able to refresh my memory if I am called to testify as to what I did, and so I can let others know the details of my involvement in the case.
Q: Have you had a chance to review your report in this case?
A: Yes.
Q: Did you find it accurate as you recalled the facts?
A: Yes.
Q: Would your testimony be more accurate if you had a chance to read your report before you testified?
A: Yes it would.
Q: Officer Kennedy, please examine your report.
(Pause while Officer Kennedy opens the folder in his lap, takes out his report, reads a page, looks at the next page for a moment, then puts the report in the folder and returns it to his lap.)
A: She said, "He has always pushed me, and this time he went too far."
Q: Thank you, Officer Kennedy.

Figure 9-1. Sample exchange between a prosecutor and an officer, showing how to use the police narrative report on the witness stand

> **Q:** Officer Johnson, I am handing you State's exhibit forty-seven. Please examine it and tell me what it is.
>
> **A:** Exhibit forty-seven is a .38 caliber Smith and Wesson revolver.
>
> **Q:** Have you ever seen it before?
>
> **A:** Yes I have.
>
> **Q:** Where?
>
> **A:** I first saw State's exhibit forty-seven in a small brown paper bag under the driver's seat of a 1975 Ford Torino.

Figure 9-2. Proper way to testify about an exhibit

Handling Exhibits

From time to time, officers on the witness stand are asked to identify physical exhibits. These physical exhibits are almost always marked with their own exhibit letter or number to distinguish them from other exhibits used in the case. The use of the exhibit letter or number is an important part of the trial. The officer should therefore refer to the physical exhibit by mentioning its exhibit letter or number during testimony about that physical exhibit.

Testifying about the exhibit by referring to it by its letter or number marks the officer as a professional, careful, and experienced witness. Jurors will rely on the testimony of witnesses whom they believe to be knowledgeable and careful about their testimony.

Typical questions by the prosecutor and answers by an officer about a particular exhibit might appear as in Figure 9-2.

Drawing on a Diagram

At times an officer will be asked to go to a large diagram in the courtroom and draw on it to better explain things to the judge or jury.

There are several things for the officer to keep in mind when faced with this task.

1. The officer should not approach the diagram unless specifically told to go to the diagram. Merely being asked if a particular object could be drawn on the diagram is not yet an invitation to do so. The officer should wait until receiving a specific direction.
2. When standing at the diagram, the officer should stand to one side so as not to block the view of the judge, jury, or attorneys.

3. When pointing at an area or object on the diagram, the officer should do so from a position at the side of the diagram, again so as not to block anyone's view of the diagram.

4. When writing on the diagram, the officer should do so from a position at the side of the diagram.

5. The writing on the diagram should only be done by the officer after having received a clear direction from the attorney to do so. In other words the officer should not jump the gun by anticipating what the attorney wants on the diagram.

6. If at all possible, when asked to label something on the diagram, the officer should write the label in letters or numbers at least one inch high so the jurors across the room can read it. The label should be written at the edge of the diagram and then a line drawn from the label to the object to which the label applies. This keeps the diagram itself as clear and understandable as possible.

These last suggestions are subject to modification by the trial prosecutor. Therefore it is always best to discuss this with the prosecutor prior to taking the witness stand.

Making Mistakes

Sooner or later every witness, including police officers, will make a mistake that will be pointed out during the actual testimony. There is only one way to handle that situation: if convinced there is a mistake in the testimony or in the police report, the officer must simply admit it without trying to explain it away. If the prosecutor wishes to have the jury hear the explanation, the prosecutor will ask questions that will give the officer an opportunity to explain. Prosecutors are often perfectly content to simply have the officer admit a mistake candidly and without hesitation, and leave it at that. This allows the prosecutor to argue very effectively that the balance of the officer's testimony is highly credible since the officer is so direct and honest about admitting errors.

SUMMARY

A police officer who testifies is usually an important witness because of the nature of the information possessed by the officer. During the investigative stage of the case, officers may collect evidence linking the suspect to the crime. They may notice important facts about the case, such as the location, position, and condition of objects. Officers may also hear suspects make comments and admissions about the crime.

An officer's testimony is expected to be clear, direct, objective, and unbiased. An officer should also be able to recall events that may be months old with a great deal of detail. The officer's police report is the most common method used by the officer to refresh memory so that the testimony is accurate, clear, and delivered with confidence.

A police officer who testifies in court is the center of attention for the period of time spent on the witness stand. The officer's words, mannerisms, and even facial expressions are noticed and analyzed. This may be an uncomfortable experience for some officers, while it is welcomed by others. Quite often the difference in how officers feel about being a witness is based on experiences they have had in being cross-examined by a defense attorney, or on horror stories they have heard about particular cases of cross-examination.

It is principally from the officer's narrative report that the defense attorney prepares for cross-examination. If the narrative report is well-organized, readable, and complete, the defense attorney naturally assumes that the officer and the investigation were thorough and complete, and that the officer will make a good witness who will be difficult to cross-examine. The defense attorney often decides to get that type of police officer off the stand quickly by asking as few questions as possible.

▼ REVIEW QUESTIONS

1. What should the police officer do in preparing for trial when an error is found in the officer's narrative report regarding that case?
2. Explain how best to approach the witness stand with the report.
3. What should the officer do on the witness stand upon wanting to review the report to refresh memory?
4. How should the officer refer to exhibits on the witness stand during testimony? Why?
5. Where should an officer stand when drawing on a diagram during the trial?
6. Upon realizing that there was a mistake made during the testimony or in the narrative report, how should the officer answer the question about the mistake?

▼ NOTES

▼

POLICE REPORT: CHECKLIST

SUMMARY
- Begin with "On."
- Be brief: time(s), date(s), name(s), addresses.
- Crime report: describe the significant event (crime); identify suspect as unknown, known, arrested.
- Follow-up report: the most significant event.

MENTIONED
- Names of persons and status (victim, suspect, etc.).
- Locate information: only if necessary.

ACTION TAKEN
- Begin with "On."
- Dispatch and arrival times and date.
- Chronological order: give reasons.
- Statements mentioned briefly.
- Physical exhibits mentioned briefly.

STATEMENTS
- Witness: "told me"; story format; do not quote.
- Suspect: date, time, place, who was present, and Miranda rights and response (or reasons not custodial); paragraph #2—"told me"; may quote.

EVIDENCE
- Four-column format.
- All columns filled in.
- All physical exhibits listed.

ACTION RECOMMENDED
- Anything left to do.
- If nothing left to do, write "None."

Eyewitness Interview

- Detailed description.
- Eyewitness's ability to observe.
- Memory aid/diagram statement.
- "Will you be able to recognize . . . ?"

Diagrams

- Purposes: crime scene; witness statement; suspect interview.

Photo Display Preparation

- Mount photos permanently.
- Use photographs of similar appearing people.
- Use photographs with similar background.
- Cover date and/or height marks on photo.
- Number the photos.

Photo Display Procedure

- Repeat the three cautionary warnings.
- Show display (discreetly note actual time).
- Report response.
- Show photocopy of display (date, time, eyewitness signature, eyewitness time estimate).
- Do not disclose outcome to eyewitness.

Photocopies to Enhance Report

- Copy significant physical evidence and attach.
- Copy important documentary evidence.

APPENDIX B

▼

POLICE REPORT: NARRATIVE EXAMPLE

SUMMARY

On August 6, 19—, at about 8:45 P.M. Arlene Virginia Quinnette was stabbed and robbed in the parking lot of the Sav-Mor Drugstore, 11413 N. Benson Street, Bay City. Troy Ernest Cohran was arrested.

MENTIONED

ARLENE VIRGINIA QUINNETTE, victim

TROY ERNEST COHRAN, suspect

PAUL A. ABBOTT, ambulance attendant

KARIN C. KOLB, ambulance attendant

LOWELL GEORGE EPSTEIN, eyewitness, will be moving in September from address on facesheet to attend the University of Michigan. He can be reached through his parents, Mr. and Mrs. Earl Epstein, 817 Elm Court, Vernonia, work phone: 632-8181, home phone: 632-2111.

OTIS LANCE MIXER, witness

ACTION TAKEN

On August 6, 19—, at 8:53 P.M. I was dispatched to the Sav-Mor Drugstore concerning an assault. I arrived at 9:02 P.M. I saw an elderly woman, later identified as Arlene Virginia Quinnette, on the ground in the parking lot. She was unconscious and appeared to have a stab wound to her upper chest area. She was being helped by ambulance attendants.

Mr. Epstein came up to me and said he'd seen the assault and had called 911. He said a man struck Mrs. Quinnette and ran off with her purse toward the south. I interviewed Mr. Epstein and obtained a diagram statement from him while the ambulance attendants took Mrs. Quinnette to the hospital. I took photographs of the scene and seized a switchblade knife that was under a car near where Mrs. Quinnette had been lying. The knife had what appeared to be blood on the blade next to the handle.

I followed the path of travel Mr. Epstein said the man took when he fled. I found Mrs. Quinnette's purse, contents, and identification scattered in the bushes at the south end of the parking lot. I began driving through the neighborhood areas south and east of the Sav-Mor Drugstore. At about 10:35 P.M. I was southbound on Monroe Street approaching 13th Street and saw a man walking south. He fit the description given me by Mr. Epstein. This was approximately two and one-half miles south and east of the Sav-Mor Drugstore. The man turned and looked at me and ran to 13th Street where he turned east. I lost sight of him for about ten seconds, and when I turned the corner, he was gone.

I parked and walked east on 13th Street. I went about one-half block to where Paul Mixer was sitting on a bus stop bench. Mr. Mixer pointed to some bushes nearby. I looked and found the man I had been chasing, hiding in the bushes. After I got him out of the bushes, he identified himself as Troy Ernest Cohran. During this time Mr. Mixer came up to us and handed me a wallet, saying he'd found it in the bushes where Mr. Cohran had been. The wallet contained some money and identification and credit cards belonging to Arlene Virginia Quinnette. Mr. Cohran blurted out, "I didn't mean to hurt her." I placed Mr. Cohran in the back of my patrol car and advised him of his Miranda rights and then interviewed him.

I lodged Mr. Cohran in jail and seized his shirt, which appeared to have bloodstains on it. While at the jail, I noticed that Mr. Cohran had no wounds or scratches on his body, leading me to conclude that the blood was probably from Mrs. Quinnette's wound.*

STATEMENTS

TROY ERNEST COHRAN, suspect. I interviewed Mr. Cohran on August 6, 19—, at 10:42 P.M. in my patrol car on 13th Street at Monroe. We were alone. I advised him of his Miranda rights and he said, "Sure do," when I asked him if he understood his rights. Mr. Cohran told me that the wallet Mr. Mixer gave me was "the old lady's wallet." I asked him how she got hurt, and he said, "She just ran up to me and began hitting me." He said that as he was trying to push her away, she accidentally cut herself on the knife he had. I asked him how he happened to have her wallet, and he was silent for about ten seconds. Then he said, "I think I want a lawyer." I did not interview him any further.

LOWELL GEORGE EPSTEIN told me that he was working part-time at Volume Discounts next to Sav-Mor Drugstore and was walking to his car in the parking lot at about 8:45 P.M. when he saw Mrs. Quinnette in the next aisle over. He heard her cry out and looked over to see a man pulling her between two cars. The man struck her several times and she fell down as the man ran off south with her purse.

Mr. Epstein said he got a good look at the man as it was still light and he was only about twenty-five feet away. The man was about 5'6", about 140 lbs., and had on an orange T-shirt with some black printing and a picture on the front. He wore grey shorts and black and white tennis shoes. He had short, dark hair and was clean-shaven. He was in his mid-twenties. The man had an earring of some kind in his right ear.

Mr. Epstein said he thought he'd be able to recognize the man if he saw him again.

Later on that day at about 11:45 P.M. Mr. Epstein came to the police department at my request. I told him I was going to show him some photographs and that the person he saw may or may not be among the photographs but to look at them carefully and tell me if he recognized anyone. He looked at them and identified Mr. Cohran. I had him circle the picture on a photocopy of the photo display of the man he saw assault Mrs. Quinnette, and date and sign it. He estimated the time it took him to make an identification as thirty seconds.

I thanked Mr. Epstein and had him go home without having told him that he had picked the man we had in custody.

EVIDENCE

ITEM	LOCATION	SEIZED BY	DISPOSITION
photocopy of photo display	police station	myself	PIC 84762, item 1
switch-blade knife	Sav-Mor parking lot	myself	same, item 4

photographs	Sav-Mor parking lot	myself	same, item 5
victim's purse, contents, and identification	bushes at end of Sav-Mor parking lot	myself	same, items 8, 9, 10
crime scene diagram	Sav-Mor parking lot	myself	same, item 6
Epstein's diagram statement	Sav-Mor parking lot	myself	same, item 3
victim's wallet	bushes on 13th near Monroe St.	Mr. Mixer and myself	same, item 7
suspect's shirt	jail	myself	same, item 11
photo display	police station	myself	same, item 2

ACTION RECOMMENDED

Fingerprint knife, purse, and contents, and compare with Mr. Cohran's fingerprints. Get sample of Mrs. Quinnette's blood and compare with blood on suspect's shirt and on the knife.

* I then put together a photo display which included a photograph of Mr. Cohran and called Mr. Epstein to come down to the police station to see if he could identify Mrs. Quinnette's assailant. He came down on August 6, 19—, at 11:45 P.M. and picked the picture of Mr. Cohran in eighteen seconds, saying, "That's the guy right there." Mr. Epstein circled the picture of Mr. Cohran on a photocopy of the photo display.

APPENDIX C

▼

WRITTEN EXERCISES

▼ EXERCISE ONE

Assignment
Write a personal letter to your friend explaining the latest call you handled as a police officer.

Facts
You were dispatched to a pizza restaurant concerning a disturbance. Upon arrival you found that a customer was demanding his money back because his pizza was burned. The owner refused and wanted the customer removed because he was loud, vulgar, and drunk. While you were talking to the owner, the customer picked up a full pitcher of beer and threw it at the owner. It missed him and shattered a large mirror and several glasses next to the mirror. The customer loudly threatened the owner as you arrested the customer and took him to jail.

Objectives
To demonstrate an ability to
1. Avoid jargon.
2. Use short, simple, direct words.
3. Avoid passive voice.
4. Use specific, rather than general words.
5. Refer to time correctly.
6. Refer to people correctly.
7. Quote appropriately.
8. Write conclusions correctly ("at the owner" is a conclusion that must be supported by reporting facts).

Grading
The letter will be graded on the choice of words used to describe the event and on the facts included in the letter to support the conclusion.

▼ EXERCISE TWO

Assignment
Write a personal letter to a friend about the report writing class you are taking. In the letter explain to your friend how to write a narrative police report in the six-section format. The letter should include such sufficient detail that, with your directions, your friend would be able to write a reasonably complete narrative police report.

Objectives
To demonstrate an ability to
1. Write clearly and simply.
2. Explain the six-section narrative format.

Grading
The letter will be graded on the thoroughness and clarity of the explanation.

▼ EXERCISE THREE

Assignment
Write a complete narrative report concerning your investigation of the following shoplifting incident:
1. People involved
   Frances Carstens, store security
   Donald Shallenberg, shoe clerk
   Viola Unwinner, suspect
2. Place of crime
   Barton's Shoes, 437 S. Blade Street, West Linn
3. Date/time (crime)
   January 27, 19—, 3:35 P.M.

Facts
Ms. Carstens was on duty in plainclothes when she saw Ms. Unwinner enter the store. Ms. Carstens, believing that she recognized Ms. Unwinner from a "Shoplifter Beware" flyer, watched and eventually saw her go to a shelf at the rear of the store, select a pair of new shoes from a box, and put them on. She then saw Ms. Unwinner put her old shoes into the box, which she then replaced on the shelf. Ms. Unwinner left the store and was stopped in the parking lot by Ms. Carstens who led her back into the store and called the police.

Upon your arrival, you met Ms. Carstens, learned what happened, and then introduced yourself to Ms. Unwinner who identified herself but told you she didn't want to talk about it. Ms. Carstens had possession of the new shoes she saw Ms. Unwinner take. Ms. Carstens asked Donald Shallenberg to get the shoe box from the shelf with Ms. Unwinner's old shoes in it. Mr. Shallenberg did so and handed the box with the old shoes to you. Ms. Carstens identified the old shoes as being the ones worn by Ms. Unwinner.

You cited Ms. Unwinner and released her. Ms. Carstens kept the new shoes and the old shoes plus the shoe box as evidence in the store's evidence locker. You learned from Mr. Shallenberg that he will be moving to the city of Monroe in the next ten days to live with his uncle.

Objective
1. To demonstrate an ability to write a report in the six-section narrative format with particular emphasis on the <u>MENTIONED</u> and the <u>EVIDENCE</u> sections.

Grading
The report will be graded on the correctness of the narrative, the content of the sections, and the language used.

▼ EXERCISE FOUR

Assignment
Write a complete narrative report concerning your investigation of the following assault incident:
1. People involved
   William Allen, suspect
   Juanita Allen, victim, suspect's wife
   Dennis Gass, victim's father
   Julius Manners, ambulance attendant
   Sheila Ward, ambulance attendant
2. Location of crime
   9168 S. Reedway Street, Metolius
3. Date/time (crime)
   August 4, 19—, between 4:30 P.M. and 7:15 P.M.

Facts

Mr. Gass is Juanita's father and knows that she and her husband William have been having domestic problems for several months. They separated a week ago, and Mr. Allen had moved out of their house on S. Reedway.

On August 4, 19—, at 4:30 P.M., Mr. Gass called his daughter on the phone and told her that he was going to bring her a piece of cheesecake her mother had made. Mr. Gass arrived at 7:15 P.M., and when there was no answer at the front door, he went to the rear door and saw that it was broken in. He went in and saw that the kitchen table was askew and the chairs were not in their proper places. One chair was lying on its side. Mr. Gass looked through the house, finding his daughter on the floor in the bathroom unconscious and bleeding from a head wound. Mr. Gass called 911.

You got the call at 7:21 P.M. and arrived at 7:31 P.M. to find the ambulance crew working on Mrs. Allen. Mr. Gass was in the front yard. Mr. Gass explained what he found and led you into the house where you saw the back doorjamb splintered and broken inwards, shattering the door casing at the strike plate. You noticed the kitchen table and chairs in disarray. In the bathroom you saw that the EMTs were about to remove Mrs. Allen to the ambulance.

You examined the kitchen more carefully and saw a sledge hammer on the floor behind the door, blood drops on the kitchen sink, and bloody prints on a glass in the sink. Closer examination of the door revealed a dent on the outside knob as if it had been hit with a heavy object. You photographed the area and seized the sledge hammer, samples of blood from the kitchen and the bathroom, and the glass.

While you were outside talking to Mr. Gass, a man drove up and Mr. Gass identified him as his daughter's husband. You introduced yourself to him and said that his wife had been injured and was at the hospital. Mr. Allen asked if you knew who broke in and did it. You asked him why he thought it was a break-in and why he thought that his wife had been injured by a person. Mr. Allen stammered and said he didn't know, he just guessed. You then noticed that Mr. Allen had a fresh cut on his hand and that he was covering it with bloody bathroom tissue. When you asked how he cut his hand, he said he was sorry he hurt his wife but she made him angry when she said she didn't want him back. He said he hit her with a metal ashtray.

You advised Mr. Allen of his Miranda rights, but he said he wanted a lawyer. You then seized the bloody tissue he was holding, as you noticed that it contained the same pattern and color as the toilet paper in the bathroom where Mrs. Allen was. You asked Mr. Gass if he would go into the house to look for the ashtray in the bathroom as you recalled seeing one on the counter. Mr. Gass did so and returned with it and handed it to you. You had told Mr. Gass to be careful and not disturb any surfaces that might contain fingerprints. Then you lodged Mr. Allen in jail for assault.

Objective
1. To demonstrate an ability to write a narrative report in the six-section narrative format with emphasis on the <u>ACTION TAKEN</u> and <u>STATEMENTS</u> sections.

Grading
The report will be graded on the correctness of the narrative and the language chosen.

▼ EXERCISE FIVE

Assignment
Write a complete narrative report concerning your investigation of the following robbery crime:
1. People involved
   Fred Kaufman, victim
   Sheila Remsick, witness
2. Location of crime
   4751 E. Washington Street, Canby
3. Date/time (crime)
   October 15, 19—, 5:15 P.M.

Facts
Sheila Remsick is the co-owner of a women's secondhand apparel shop next door to the Shur-way gas station where Fred Kaufman pumps gas. On October 15, 19—, at 5:15 P.M. Mrs. Remsick walked out of her back door as her delivery boy had not yet returned and she was looking for him. She happened to look next door in time to see Mr. Kaufman walk up to an orange van with brown primer spots on its left front end parked at one of the gas pumps. She then saw Mr. Kaufman walk around the front of the van as if to go to one of the gas pumps and saw the van's driver get out and follow Mr. Kaufman.

She turned away for a moment or two. She then heard a loud shout and a "thump" noise and looked back in time to see the van driver get in the van and drive off. As the van drove off, it passed within twenty feet of Mrs. Remsick. The driver stopped the van, looked at her, and said, "If you ever say I was here, I'll hunt you down and kill you." Then he drove off.

The man was in his mid-twenties and wore a black T-shirt under a green and black plaid shirt. He had black hair cut short and a mustache and small goatee. He was about 5'10" and 170 lbs.

Mrs. Remsick looked over and saw that Mr. Kaufman was lying on the ground next to the gas pumps. She went to him and saw that he was bleeding from an apparent chest wound. She called 911 at 5:23 P.M. You were dispatched at that time and arrived at the gas station at 5:32 P.M.

You noticed that Mr. Kaufman was being given emergency medical aid by ambulance attendants for what appeared to be a stab wound. You also noticed that a chain attached to Mr. Kaufman's belt, typically attached to a wallet, was cut and the wallet was gone. You found a partial link on the ground next to Mr. Kaufman. You interviewed Mrs. Remsick and got a description of the van and of its driver. She said she thought she could recognize the driver of the van if she were to see him again.

Objective
1. To demonstrate an ability to write a narrative report in the six-section format with emphasis on the correct way to interview an eyewitness to a crime.

Grading
The report will be graded on the correctness of the narrative, the content of the section, and the language used.

▼ EXERCISE SIX

Assignment
Write a complete narrative report concerning a follow-up investigation of the Shur-way gas station robbery described in Exercise Five. In the investigation the following facts were learned:

1. People involved
   Thomas Waters
2. Location of arrest
   7171 Morgandale Road, Durkee
3. Date/time (event)
   October 16, 19—, 2:30 P.M.

Facts

On October 16, 19—, Officer Tommy Pahrmar, who worked the night shift, told you as you came on shift that he recalled stopping an orange van with a brown primered front end three nights ago. The driver was Thomas Waters of 631 'B' Lynwood Court, Durkee. He made the traffic stop just one mile from the Shur-way gas station.

You went to the Lynwood Court address, saw the van, and realized it fit the description given by the eyewitness, Sheila Remsick. While you were watching the van, a male came out of the apartment complex at 2:30 P.M. and got into the van and drove away. The man fit the description given by Mrs. Remsick perfectly. You stopped the van in front of 7171 Morgandale Road, Durkee, and made a probable cause arrest of the driver, Thomas Waters. You searched the van because you believed it may have contained the stolen wallet, its contents, and a tool to cut a wallet chain since the robbery had taken place only the day before. You found a severed chain link that appeared to match the chain on Mr. Kaufman's belt at the time he was assaulted the day before. You found the link on the floor between the front bucket seats of the van and a wallet belonging to Mr. Kaufman in the glove compartment of the van.

In an interview room at the jail, about forty-five minutes after the arrest, you advised Mr. Waters of his Miranda rights. He answered, "Yeah," when you asked if he understood the rights. You asked him if he had the van on the evening of the 15th, and he said, "Nobody else drives my van." When you explained that his vehicle had been involved in an armed robbery the evening before and that an eyewitness saw the whole thing, he said, "It wasn't me." Then you told Mr. Waters that the wallet and part of the chain were found in his van. He was silent for about ten seconds and said that he got in a fight with "the guy" when he made Mr. Waters mad, but that he didn't steal any wallet.

You asked him how he came to have the wallet and he said, "I want a lawyer." You ended the interview with him at that point and lodged him in jail.

Objective

1. To demonstrate an ability to write the six-section format with emphasis on the suspect interview.

Grading

The report will be graded on the correctness of the narrative, the content of the sections, and the language used.

▼ EXERCISE SEVEN

Assignment

Prepare a proper basic sketched diagram of the kitchen area of your residence. Complete the diagram as if it were a crime scene diagram.
Include the following

1. A bloody palm print on a wall next to a light switch
2. A pool of blood on the floor
3. A bloody knife in the sink
4. Drops of blood on the floor
5. A knit stocking cap on the floor under the kitchen table
6. A crumpled up bill of sale for a 1987 Honda on top of the stove

Objectives

To demonstrate the knowledge and ability to

1. Prepare a proper basic sketched diagram of both a room's floor plan and a vertical wall in that room.
2. Use the basic diagram as a crime scene diagram.
3. Complete the legend section of a crime scene diagram properly.

Grading

The crime scene diagram will be graded on the correctness of the sketch and the items drawn on it, of what is written on the diagram, and of what is written in the legend section.

▼ EXERCISE EIGHT

Assignment

Prepare a proper basic sketched diagram of an actual outside area around your residence, a school, or a friend's residence. Complete the diagram as if it were a statement from an eyewitness to an assault.

The eyewitness you interview using this diagram is Paul Soto. He told you that he was walking home from work through the area depicted in your sketch when he saw a short, bald man in a parked pickup truck open the passenger door and fall out onto the ground moaning.

Mr. Soto was about fifty feet from the short, bald man. Light from nearby (lamppost or porch) lit up the area. As Mr. Soto went to him, another man got out of the driver's side and told Mr. Soto, "Get the hell out of here. This is none of your business." Then the man walked toward Mr. Soto and raised his right hand, getting within ten feet of him. Mr. Soto saw what he thought was a knife in the man's right hand, so Mr. Soto left and called 911.

He noticed that the man who had gotten out of the driver's side of the pickup was in his early thirties and had very dark hair, trimmed short and slightly wavy. The man was about 5'10" and 160 lbs. and wore glasses with a slight tint to them. He had on a light blue knit shirt and faded denim trousers.

Objectives
To demonstrate the knowledge and ability to
1. Prepare a proper basic sketched diagram of an outside area.
2. Use the basic diagram as a statement from an eyewitness.
3. Complete the legend section of such a diagram.

Grading
The witness statement diagram will be graded on the correctness of the sketch and the items drawn on it, of what is written on the diagram, and of what is written in the legend section.

▼ EXERCISE NINE

Assignment
Prepare a proper basic sketched diagram of the crime scene at the Shur-way gas station in Exercise Five.

Facts
Use the same facts about the interview with Mr. Waters as described in Exercise Six, but include the following additional facts for the purpose of this assignment:

You told Mr. Waters that you had searched his van and he replied, "OK, I got in a fight with the guy. He made me mad, but I didn't steal any wallet." You asked him how he knew a wallet was stolen and he said, "Well, I did take it but only because I was angry at the guy." He then said, "I had the knife and he just ran into it."

You showed him the crime scene diagram and asked where he was and where the guy was when the guy ran into the knife. Mr. Waters made a mark on the diagram to indicate where he was and a second mark to show where Mr. Kaufman was at the time of the stabbing. You completed writing on the diagram, and Mr. Waters placed his initials in the appropriate places and then signed and dated the diagram.

Objectives
To demonstrate the knowledge and ability to
1. Prepare a proper basic sketched diagram.
2. Use the basic diagram in an interview with a suspect.
3. Complete the legend section of such a diagram.

Grading
The suspect interview diagram will be graded on the correctness of the sketch and of the items drawn on it, of what is written on the diagram, and of what is written in the legend section.

▼ EXERCISE TEN

Assignment
Prepare a proper photo display mounted permanently in a file folder. Include six photos of similarly appearing men. (You may use pictures of men from a periodical of your choice.) Prepare a photocopy of the original photo display and make the appropriate marks and writings on the copy as if you had shown it to Sheila Remsick (Exercise Five) on October 16, 19—, at 6:45 P.M. She recognized the suspect in what she believed to be about ten seconds.

Objectives
To demonstrate the knowledge and ability to
1. Prepare a proper photo display.
2. Use a photocopy of that display in an interview with an eyewitness who has made an identification from that photo display.

Grading

The original and the photocopy of the photo display will be graded on their appearance of uniformity and fairness, and on what is written on the photocopy.

▼ EXERCISE ELEVEN

Assignment

Write a narrative report by rewriting the following report. Use the same facts as given, adding only those facts that are necessary for a proper narrative report.

Summary: On July 27, 19—, writer investigated a theft of jewelry at THOMPKINS' JEWELRY STORE, 4763 Broadway, Beaver, Oregon. The jewelry was recovered and an arrest was effected.

Mentioned:

Bernard Thompkins, (R/P)

Robert C. Collins, (W)

James Alan Colquist, suspect

Action Taken: R/P THOMPKINS reported that he had been robbed of watches and rings. Writer responded to R/P's establishment at 0841 hours and learned that a white male app. mid-twenties, thin build, light blue, wrinkled, ill-fitting suit, red and yellow shirt, appr. 6'1" and wearing black sandals with white socks, entered R/P's establishment just as it was opened for business and asked to see some expensive men's watches and women's diamond rings. SUSPECT told R/P that he had just inherited a large sum of money from his grandfather and wanted to buy himself an expensive watch and his girlfriend a diamond ring. Just as R/P placed a tray of watches and a tray of rings on the display counter, SUSPECT grabbed a handful of watches and a handful of rings and made exit utilizing the front door. R/P then called 911 at 0836 hours. Upon arrival it was learned that upon SUSPECT's exit from the store, witness COLLINS observed SUSPECT being pursued by victim THOMPKINS indicating that SUSPECT had just stolen jewelry causing witness COLLINS to commence foot pursuit of SUSPECT and follow him to Maryhurst Park where he terminated the pursuit. After getting SUSPECT's physical description from COLLINS, writer had COLLINS write the description on a piece of paper and date and sign it. Writer then proceeded to Maryhurst Park and at about 1049 hours observed a white male in his mid-twenties wearing light blue trousers and a red and yellow flower print short-sleeved shirt. He was sitting on a park bench near the entrance to the Japanese Gardens. The man was thin and had on black sandals over white socks. There was a light blue jacket folded over the back of the bench next to the man. Writer approached and the man stood up and walked behind the bench and toward the horse riding trails. Writer ordered SUSPECT to stop and placed him under arrest, frisked him finding no jewelry, placed him in writer's patrol unit, and advised him of his Miranda rights. He identified himself as JAMES ALAN COLQUIST. Writer then visually examined the area and physically located a popcorn box with seven diamond rings and five watches in it. They were found about six feet behind the park bench where SUSPECT COLQUIST had been sitting. The box was open and upright on the grass and the jewelry was plainly visible inside. An eighth ring was discovered under the park bench. Writer then asked SUSPECT COLQUIST at about 1109 hours if the jewelry was his. He indicated that it was not, that he had never seen the popcorn box before. Writer advised that the box would be fingerprinted to see if SUSPECT COLQUIST had touched it, and SUSPECT COLQUIST indicated that he may have touched it. Writer then advised SUSPECT COLQUIST that he should not complicate his situation by lying. SUSPECT COLQUIST then said something to me that made me believe he had stolen the jewelry. Writer then had witness ROBT COLLINS respond to writer's location and upon arrival, writer advised ROBT that writer was going to have him visually observe an individual that may or may not have been the one who stole the jewelry but to view him to see if he was familiar. ROBT, in three seconds, positively identified SUSPECT COLQUIST who was in custody in the rear of writer's patrol unit. Writer then lodged SUSPECT in the city jail and returned to the R/P with the jewelry and a photo display with SUSPECT's photo being number four. R/P at 1331 hours positively identified SUSPECT in photo in twelve seconds as the one who stole the property and positively identified all the jewelry and rings as his. Writer took photographs of the rings and watches and returned them to the R/P.

Statements:

BERNARD THOMPKINS. R/P advises that the recovered jewelry is his and that photo number four is the one who stole his jewelry. (R/P) advised that as he opened his store, the SUSPECT came into the store and asked to look at jewelry as he had just inherited some money. SUSPECT then stole a handful of rings and a handful of watches from their display cases and exited the store.

ROBERT COLLINS: (W) stated that he bumped into a man running from the store and followed the man to Maryhurst Park. ROBT advised that he will be moving in the next few weeks to live with his sister, Edna Polumns, who lives at 2122 W. Barthmore Court, Los Angeles, California, phone 719-212-0416.

Evidence:

I seized six rings and five watches from a popcorn box. I photographed and returned them to the R/P. I kept the popcorn box for printing. I also placed in evidence a photo display that I'd shown to the R/P, as well as a photocopy on which the R/P had indicated photo number four. Piece of paper on which witness COLLINS had written a description of the man he'd followed to the park. Diagram statement obtained from R/P. Crime scene diagram.

<u>Action Recommended:</u>

That R/P hire a security officer for his store. Also have the popcorn box printed and compare any latent prints with those of SUSPECT COLQUIST.

Objective

1. To demonstrate the knowledge and ability to correctly arrange information obtained during a field investigation into a well-written narrative report.

Grading

The report will be graded on the proper writing of each of the six sections of the narrative, and on using the correct format. Language choices will also be graded.

INDEX